Fish of Michigan
FIELD GUIDE

by David Bosanko

Adventure Publications, Inc.
Cambridge, MN

rs

Special thanks to the U.S. Fish and Wildlife Service, and the Michigan and Minnesota Departments of Natural Resources.

Edited by Dan Johnson

Cover and book design by Jonathan Norberg

Photo/Illustration credits by artist and page number:
Cover illustrations: Brook Trout (main) by Duane Raver/USFWS; Bluegill (upper) by Joseph Tomelleri
Timothy Knepp/USFWS: 88 (top), 90, 102, 104 **MI DNR:** 26 **MN DNR:** 24, 25 **MyFWC.com/fishing:** 29 **Joseph Tomelleri:** 27 (top), 44 (both), 46, 58, 60, 62, 64, 68 (main, right inset), 70 (all), 74 (main), 76, 78 (both), 82, 86, 88 (bottom), 92 (inset 7), 94 (bottom), 96 (main, inset 1), 100, 106, 108, 110 (main, insets), 112, 114, 116 (both), 118, 122, 124, 126, 128, 142, 150, 158 **Duane Raver/USFWS:** 19, 27 (bottom), 32, 34, 36, 38, 40 (all), 42, 48, 50, 52, 54, 56, 66, 74, (second inset), 80, 84, 92, 94 (top), 98, 120, 130, 132, 134, 136, 138, 140, 144, 146, 148, 152, 154, 156 **WI DNR:** 24 (lower right)

10 9 8 7 6 5 4 3 2 1

Copyright 2007 by David Bosanko
Published by Adventure Publications, Inc.
820 Cleveland St. S
Cambridge, MN 55008
1-800-678-7006
www.adventurepublications.net
Printed in China
ISBN-13: 978-1-59193-193-5
ISBN-10: 1-59193-193-2

TABLE OF CONTENTS

Primary References 166
Index 167
About the Author 174

HOW TO USE THIS BOOK

Your Fish of Michigan field guide is designed to make it easy to identify more than 70 species of the most common and important fish in Michigan, and learn fascinating facts about each species' range, natural history and more.

The fish are organized by families (such as Catfish, Minnow, Perch, Pike, Salmon and Sunfish), which are listed in alphabetical order. Within these families, individual species are also arranged alphabetically, in groups where necessary. For example, members of the Sunfish family are divided into Black Bass, Crappie and True Sunfish groups. For a detailed list of fish families and individual species, turn to the Table of Contents (pg. 3); the Index (pp. 167-173) provides a handy reference guide to fish by common name (such as Lake Trout) and other common terms for the species.

Fish Identification

Determining a fish's body shape is the first step to identifying it. Each fish family usually exhibits one or sometimes two basic outlines. Catfish have long, stout bodies with flattened heads, barbels or "whiskers" around the mouth, a relatively tall but narrow dorsal fin, and an adipose fin. There are two forms of sunfish: the flat, round, plate-like outline we see in Bluegills; and the torpedo or "fusiform" shape of bass.

In this field guide you can quickly identify your catch by first matching its general body shape to one of the fish family silhouettes listed in the Table of Contents (pp. 3-7). From there, turn to that family's section and use the illustrations and text descriptions to identify your fish. A Sample Page (pg. 30) is provided to explain how the information is presented in each two-page spread.

For some species, the illustration will be enough to identify your catch, but it is important to note that your fish may not look exactly like the picture. Fish frequently change colors. Males that are brightly colored during the spawning season may be dull silver at other times. Likewise, bass caught in muddy streams show much less pattern than those taken from clear lakes—and all fish lose some of their markings and color when they are removed from the water.

Most fish are similar in appearance to one or more other species—often, but not always, within the same family. For example, the Black Crappie is remarkably similar to its cousin the White Crappie. To accurately identify such look-alikes, check the inset illustrations and accompanying notes below the main illustration, under the "Similar Species" heading.

Throughout Fish of Michigan, we use basic biological and fisheries management terms that refer to physical characteristics or conditions of fish and their environment, such as dorsal fin or turbid water. For your convenience, these terms are defined in the Glossary (pp. 160-165), along with other handy fish-related terms and their definitions.

ABOUT MICHIGAN FISH

Michigan possesses four times more water than any other of the 48 contiguous states. There are 3,000 miles of Great Lakes coastline, 11,000 inland lakes and 36,000 miles of rivers and streams. The large diversity of waters provides an almost unlimited number of habitats for freshwater fish—and a profusion of opportunities to watch, study and pursue them.

There are approximately 154 species of fish in Michigan. Of these, thirty are the primary targets of fishermen. Another 40-plus species are of particular interest to those who spend time near the water, either because of their status as prized baitfish, their unique characteristics or the likelihood you'll see them on forays to various freshwater habitats. Together, these species provide an introduction to Michigan's major fish families.

FREQUENTLY ASKED QUESTIONS
What is a fish?
Fish are aquatic, cold-blooded animals with backbones, gills and fins.

Are all fish cold-blooded?
All freshwater fish are cold-blooded. Recently it has been discovered that some members of the saltwater tuna family are warm-blooded. Whales and dolphins are also warm-blooded, but they are mammals, not fish.

Do all fish have scales?
Most fish have scales that look like the ones found on the common goldfish. A few, like gar, have scales that resemble armor plates. Some, such as catfish, have no scales at all.

indicates hard-bottom spawning areas, often in bulrush beds; **dark green** highlights summertime areas; **brown** shows fall locations; and **light blue** indicates areas crappies are found from first-ice in December through March. Keep in mind that crappies (like many other species) often rise and fall in the water column in response to light levels and prey location. Depending on the food source and other factors, crappies will move closer to the surface at dawn, dusk and during the night, and drop close to bottom during the day.

Habitat such as aquatic vegetation also plays a major role in the location of many species throughout the year. For example, research has shown a strong correlation between healthy stands of vegetation and the summertime location of Blackchin Shiners—an important forage fish also considered an "indicator species" because it is sensitive to habitat degradation. Since these shiners favor the same habitat as juvenile game fish, any declines in the shiner population should be of great concern to anglers.

By studying a species' habitat, food and reproduction information in this book—and understanding how it interacts with other Michigan fish—it is possible to make an educated prediction of where to find it in any lake or river.

FISH NAMES

A Walleye is a Walleye in Michigan, where it's revered as a game fish. But in the northern parts of its range, Canadians call it a *jack* or *jackfish*. And in the eastern United States it is often grouped with other pike-shaped fish and called a *pickerel* or *walleyed pike*.

Because common names may vary regionally, and even change for different sizes of the same species, scientific names are used that are exactly the same around the world. Each species has only one correct scientific name that can be recognized anywhere, in any language. The Walleye is *Sander vitreus* from Madison to Moscow.

Scientific names are made up of Greek or Latin words that often describe the species. There are two parts to a scientific name, the generic or "genus," which is capitalized (*Sander*), and the specific name, which is not capitalized (*vitreus*). Scientific names are displayed in *italic* text. A species' genus represents a group of closely related fish. The Walleye and the Sauger are in the same genus, so they share the generic name *Sander*. But each have different specific names, *vitreus* for Walleye, *canadenses* for the Sauger. Thus the full scientific name for Walleye is *Sander vitreus* and *Sander canadenses* for the Sauger.

It is inappropriate to use the specific name without its accompanying generic name, as many species have the same specific name. Saugers and Canada geese share similar specific names. Without knowing the genus of your catch, it would be hard to know if it should be plucked or scaled.

FUN WITH FISH

There are many ways to enjoy Michigan's fish, from reading about them in this book to watching them in the wild—including donning a dive mask and jumping in; wearing polarized glasses to observe them from above the surface; or using an underwater camera to monitor fish behavior during the open-water period and through the ice.

Hands-on activities are also popular. Most children and more than a few adults enjoy wading the shallows, catching small fish and other aquatic critters with a minnow net, bucket or their bare hands. Always read and follow Michigan's fishing regulations.

RECREATIONAL FISHING

The fishing opportunities in Michigan are incredibly numerous and diverse. From trout and salmon in the Great Lakes to bluegills off the dock—and nearly everything in between—we have it. Proceeds from license sales, along with special taxes anglers pay on fishing supplies and motorboat fuel, fund the majority of DNR fish management efforts, including fish surveys, the development of special regulations, and stocking programs. The sport also has a huge impact on Michigan's economy, supporting thousands of jobs in fishing, tourism and related industries.

LEARNING TO FISH

Learning to fish can be intimidating, especially if you have no one to teach you. Fortunately, help is available. One source is the DNR, which offers a wealth of information to help new anglers throughout the state. A variety of educational materials are available on the DNR website. In addition, a number of state and local fishing organizations, sportsmen's clubs and church groups hold events that teach people to fish.

SHARING THE SPORT

Veteran anglers are a valuable resource for teaching new anglers to fish. Of today's 50 million anglers in the United States, 99 percent say they fish because someone once took the time to introduce them to the sport. As American lifestyles change, however, fewer people (especially youths) have access to a parent or grandparent as fishing mentors.

Recent research found that fathers have diminishing role as fishing mentors. Among the 67 percent of respondents who said "dad" took them on their first fishing trip, 87.8 percent were 35 years of age or older, compared to only 12.2 percent for those under 35. Perhaps as a result, U.S. children today spend an average of 44 hours a week experiencing life through a glass—watching TV, playing video games and on the computer.

That is why the Recreational Boating and Fishing Foundation (RBFF), a non-profit organization charged by congressional action to address declining fishing participation, created a new program called Anglers' Legacy. The goal is to rally the country's estimated 7.5 million most avid anglers to introduce at least one new person to fishing per year. For details, visit AnglersLegacy.org.

FISH MANAGEMENT

The DNR uses a variety of methods to manage Michigan's fish, including habitat protection and improvement; fish stocking; and gathering information through scientific surveys of fish populations, habitat and fishing activity.

The DNR also adjusts the fishing regulations to prevent overharvest. As anglers have become more proficient, thanks to expanded knowledge and better equipment, fishing regulations have become more complex, particularly with the addition of special length, slot and bag limits. Management increasingly is on a lake-by-lake basis, as well, allowing fish managers to tailor the rules to enhance individual fisheries. Fortunately, fishing regulation handbooks are readily available wherever fishing licenses are sold, and on the DNR website. It is up to the responsible angler to help preserve fish populations. Please do your part and play by the rules.

CATCH-AND-RELEASE FISHING

The practices of selective harvest (keeping some fish to eat and releasing the rest) and total catch-and-release fishing allow anglers to enjoy the sport without harming the resource. Catch-and-release is especially important with certain species and sizes of fish, and in lakes or rivers where biologists are trying to improve the fishery by protecting large predators or breeding age, adult fish. The fishing regulations, DNR website and your local DNR fisheries office are excellent sources of advice on which fish to keep and which to release.

In virtually all Michigan fisheries, trophy fish of every species are treasures too rare to be caught only once. Photographs and graphite replicas are ethical alternatives to killing a trophy fish simply for the purpose of displaying it.

FISH HANDLING TIPS

Catch-and-release is only truly successful if the fish survives the experience. Following are helpful tips to help reduce the chances of post-release mortality.

- Play and land fish quickly.

- Wet your hands before touching a fish, to avoid removing its protective slime coating.

- Handle the fish gently and keep it in the water as much as possible.

- Do not hold the fish by the eye sockets or gills. Hold it by the lower lip or under the gill plate—and support its belly.

- If a fish is deeply hooked, cut the line so at least an inch hangs outside the mouth. This helps the hook lie flush when the fish takes in food.

- Circle hooks may help reduce the number of deeply hooked fish.

- Avoid fishing in deep water unless you plan to keep your catch.

- Don't plan to release fish that have been on a stringer or in a livewell.

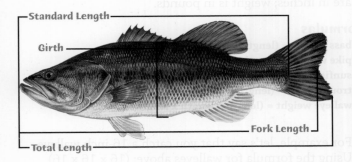

Standard Length

Girth

Fork Length

Total Length

FISH MEASUREMENT

The length of a fish is measured in three ways, standard length, fork length and total length. Standard length is used by ichthyologists (scientist who study fish). Fisheries biologists use fork length and the general public total length. The first two are more accurate as tails are often damaged or worn down in older fish. For the angler, total length is the most important as it is used in determining the legality of the catch. If you think your fish is a record catch be sure to record both the total and fork length.

LENGTH-TO-WEIGHT RATIOS

It is possible to determine the approximate weight of a fish without weighing it on a scale, (which can damage it or increase stress due to time out of the water). Using the formulas below (courtesy of the Wisconsin DNR), you can quickly determine the weight of popular game fish. Lengths are in inches; weight is in pounds.

Formulas

bass weight = (length x length x girth) / 1,200
pike weight = (length x length x length) / 3,500
sunfish weight = (length x length x length) / 1,200
trout weight = (length x girth x girth) / 800
walleye weight = (length x length x length) / 2,700

For example, let's say that you catch a 16-inch walleye. Using the formula for walleyes above: (16 x 16 x 16) divided by 2,700 = 1.5 pounds. Your walleye would weigh approximately 1.5 pounds.

RECORD FISH

Most states, but not all, maintain lists of state record fish. National and world records are kept by the National Fresh Water Fishing Hall of Fame and the International Game Fish Association. Each organization has its own standards and procedures for recognizing record fish. The North American records used in this book are those recorded by the National Fresh Water Fishing Hall of Fame. If you think you have caught a state or world record and want to register it, follow these steps:

• Contact the organization you wish to record your fish with to acquire the correct forms and procedures.

- Measure the total and fork length of your fish. Measure the girth of fish at its largest point.

- Weigh your fish on a state-certified scale (most commercial scales).

- Have all measurements and weights witnessed and the scale certification number recorded.

- Have your fish identified at a DNR fisheries office.

- Take a clear color picture of you holding your fish.

- Keep your fish whole, either fresh or frozen.

Helpful contacts include:

Michigan Department of Natural Resources
www.dnr.state.mi.us; (517) 373-7540

National Fresh Water Fishing Hall of Fame
www.Freshwater-Fishing.org; (715) 634-4440

International Game Fish Association
www.igfa.org; (954) 927-2628

MICHIGAN MASTER ANGLER STATE RECORDS

SPECIES	WEIGHT (LBS.)	WHERE CAUGHT	YEAR
American Eel	7.44	Lake St. Clair	1990
Atlantic Salmon	32.62	Lake Michigan	1981
Black Buffalo	33.25	Grand River	2004
Black Bullhead	3.44	Magician Lake	1999
Black Crappie	4.12	Lincoln Lake	1947
Bluegill	2.75	Vaughn Lake	1983
Bowfin	14.00	Crooked lake	1981

SPECIES	WEIGHT (LBS.)	WHERE CAUGHT	YEAR
Brook Trout	9.50	Clear Lake	1996
Brown Bullhead	3.62	N/A	1989
Brown Trout	34.62	Lake Michigan	2000
Burbot	18.25	St. Mary's River	1980
Channel Catfish	40.00	Houghton Lake	1964
Chinook Salmon	46.06	Grand River	1978
Coho Salmon	30.56	Platte River	1976
Common Carp	61.50	Wolf Lake	1974
Flathead Catfish	47.50	Maple River	1943
Freshwater Drum	26.00	Muskegon Lake	1973
Gizzard Shad	4.12	Lake St. Clair	1996
Green Sunfish	1.53	Kirkwood Lake	1990
Hybrid Sunfish	1.44	Doans Lake	1991
Kokanee Salmon	1.94	Clinton River	1978
Lake Herring	5.40	Grand Traverse Bay	1992
Lake Sturgeon	193.00	Mullett Lake	1974
Lake Trout	61.50	Lake Superior	1997
Lake Whitefish	14.28	Lake Superior	1993
Largemouth Bass	11.94 (tie)	Alcona Dam/Big Pine Island L.	1959/1934
Longnose Gar	18.00	Williamsville Lake	1995
Longnose Sucker	6.88	St. Joseph River	1986
Mooneye	1.69	Lake St. Clair	1995
Muskellunge (Northern)	49.75	Thornapple Lake	2000
Muskellunge (Great Lakes)	48.00	Lake Skegemog	1984
N. Hog Sucker	2.54	St. Joseph River	1994
Northern Pike	39.00	Dodge Lake	1961
Pink Salmon	8.56	Carp River	1987
Pumpkinseed	1.35	Baw Beese Lake	2004
Quillback	8.00	Stony Lake	2000
Rainbow Trout	26.50	Lake Michigan	1975
Redear Sunfish	1.97	Thompson Lake	2002
Redhorse	12.89	Muskegon River	1991
Rock Bass	3.62	Holloway Reservoir	1965
Round Whitefish	4.06	Lake Michigan	1992

SPECIES	WEIGHT (LBS.)	WHERE CAUGHT	YEAR
Sauger	6.56	Torch Lake	1976
Smallmouth Bass	9.25	Long Lake	1906
Splake	17.50	Lake Michigan	2004
Tiger Muskie	51.19	Lac Vieux Desert	1919
Walleye	17.19	Pine River	1951
Warmouth	1.38	Great Bear Lake	2001
White Bass Hybrid	10.75	Kalamazoo River	1996
White Bass	6.44	Saginaw Bay	1989
White Crappie	3.39	Stony Creek Lake	2000
White Perch	1.88	Lake Huron	2002
White Sucker	7.19	Au Sable River	1982
Yellow Bullhead	3.60	Lake Sixteen	2003
Yellow Perch	3.75	Lake Independence	1947

FISH CONSUMPTION ADVISORIES

Fish are healthy sources of low-fat protein and important nutrients. But because most of the world's surface water contains some industrial contaminants—and Michigan's lakes and rivers are no exception—some fish contain mercury, PCBs and other harmful toxins. These can be harmful to you and your family if eaten too often, and can stay in your body for years.

The Michigan DNR and Department of Community Health have detailed information on eating fish, including advisories on fish consumption, tips on choosing fish that are lower in chemicals and health risks, and advice on how to prepare fish to further reduce risk of contaminants. Call the Department of Community Health, (800) MI-TOXIC, or visit www.michigan.gov/mdch-toxic.

FISH DISEASES

Like other living creatures, fish are susceptible to various parasites, infections and diseases. Fish are especially vulnerable when stressed by environmental factors such as rapid warming of the water temperature, and after traumatic events, including being wounded by a predator or improperly handled by an angler. Fish diseases include:

Black spot disease: Caused by tiny parasites that produce black spots resembling black pepper sprinkled on the fins or fillets. Fish that inhabit shallow water are most affected. The condition is very common throughout the state, but experts say the fish are edible if well cooked.

Heterosporis: Predominantly seen in yellow perch, the disease has also been found in walleyes, northern pike, trout-perch, burbot, pumpkinseed, sculpin and rock bass. Heterosporis is a microscopic parasite that infects muscle tissue of fish by producing millions of spores, which destroy muscle tissue. Infected areas look like white or "opaque areas" in the uncooked fish fillet. Little is known about the life cycle, but it is believed the disease may be spread by infected fathead minnows sold as bait. There is no evidence heterosporis can infect people. It is thought, but not proven; that thoroughly cooking infected fish will destroy spores.

Myofibrogranuloma: Only recorded in walleyes, it is caused by a virus and not considered infectious. Environmental conditions and genetics may play a role in its development. An affected fish looks normal externally, but areas of the fillet appear semi-translucent or yellow brown, with knotted muscle fibers. The tissue has a dry appearance and may appear granular with mineral deposits. Anglers are advised not to eat fish with this condition.

Dermal Sarcoma: Grape-like tumors only seen in walleyes. Condition produces warty growths on the fish's skin and fins. Growths are usually gray-white or pinkish in color. Infections occur any time but are more common during the spawn, when virus is spread through physical contact. Not known to affect humans; always cook fish thoroughly.

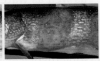

Lymphosarcoma: A cauliflower-like tumor on the skin, it is most likely caused by a virus and transmitted by physical contact. Affects muskies and northern pike; tumors range up to several inches in size, depending on water temperature. It is more prominent at cooler water temperatures, and the tumor may spread to the fish's inner organs. Consumption of affected fish not advised.

Muskie Pox (Piscirickettsia): In May of 2002 the Michigan DNR collected several muskellunge with red skin rashes from the Anchor Bay area of Lake St. Clair. It was later determined to be a *Piscirickettsia*-like organism; similar pathogens have caused increased mortality in white seabass, and *Piscirickettsia salmonis* (*P. salmonis*) causes high mortality rates in salmonid species in Norway, Chile, Ireland and Canada. To date the disease has not been linked to major affects on the Lake St. Clair muskie fishery, but DNR research is ongoing. Signs of the disease include deeply sunken eyes and red sores or rashes on the skin. Anglers who catch fish with these symptoms should contact the Mount Clemens Fisheries Research Station, (586) 465-4771.

INVASIVE SPECIES

Exotic, invasive aquatic species are a threat to native plants, fish and animals—as well as water-based recreation, particularly fishing. The invaders come in many forms, but the results are consistently negative. Eurasian Watermilfoil produces thick surface mats that crowd out native plants; the Round Goby displaces native fish; Zebra Mussels crowd out native mussels and disrupt entire lake ecosystems.

In general, cleaning your boat and emptying your livewell and minnow pail on dry land will go a long way toward slowing the spread of invasive species. Current information on specific invasive species is available from Michigan Sea Grant at www.miseagrant.umich.edu.

FISH ANATOMY

To identify fish, you will need to know a few basic terms that apply to fins and their locations.

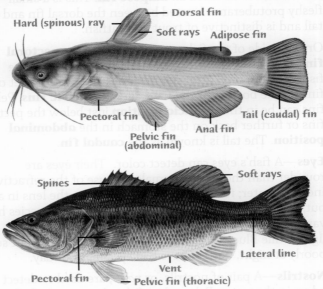

Fins are made up of bony structures that support a membrane. There are three kinds of bony structures in fins. **Soft rays** are fixable fin supports that are sometimes branched. **Spines** are stiff, often sharp supports that are not jointed. Hard rays are stiff, pointed, barbed structures that can be raised or lowered. Catfish are famous for their hard rays that are mistakenly called spines. Sunfish have soft rays associated with spines to form a dorsal fin.

Fins are named by their position on the fish. The **dorsal fin** is on the top along the midline. A few fish have another fin on their back called an **adipose fin**. This is a small fleshy protuberance located between the dorsal fin and the tail and is distinctive of trout and catfish.

On each side of the fish near the gills are the **pectoral fins**. The **anal fin** is located along the midline on the fish's bottom or ventral side. There is also a paired set of fins on the bottom of the fish called the **pelvic fins**. Pelvic fins can be in the **thoracic position** just below the pectoral fins or further back on the stomach in the **abdominal position**. The tail is known as the **caudal fin**.

Eyes—A fish's eyes can detect color. Their eyes are rounder than those of mammals because of the refractive index of water; focus is achieved by moving the lens in and out, not distorting it as in mammals. Different species have varying levels of eyesight. Walleyes can see well in low light, while Bluegills have excellent daytime vision but see poorly at night. Catfish have bad eyes night or day.

Nostrils—A pair of nostrils, or *nares*, are used to detect odors in the water. Eels and catfishes have particularly well-developed senses of smell.

Mouth—The shape of the mouth is a clue to what the fish eats. The larger the food it consumes, the larger the mouth.

Teeth—Not all fish have teeth, but those that do have mouthgear designed to help them feed. Walleyes, northern pike and muskies have sharp canine teeth for grabbing and holding prey. Minnows have *pharyngeal* teeth—located in the throat—for grinding. Catfish have *cardiform* teeth, which feel like a rough patch in the front of the mouth. Bass have tiny patches of vomerine teeth in the roof of their mouth.

Swim Bladder—Almost all fish have a swim bladder, a balloon-like organ that helps the fish regulate its buoyancy.

Lateral Line—This sensory organ helps the fish detect movement in the water (to help avoid predators or capture prey) as well as water currents and pressure changes. It consists of fluid-filled sacs with hair-like sensors, which are open to the water through a row of pores in their skin along each side—creating a visible line along the fish's side.

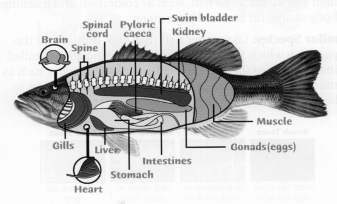

Description: brief summary of physical characteristics to help you identify the fish, such as coloration and markings, body shape, fin size and placement

Similar Species: Lists other fish that look similar and the pages on which they can be found. Also includes detailed inset drawings (below) highlighting physical traits such as markings, mouth size or shape and fin characteristics to help you distinguish this fish from similar species

Brook Trout	**Brown Trout**	**Rainbow Trout**	**Lake Trout**
worm-like markings, red spots	large dark spots, small red dots	pink stripe on silver body	sides lack red spots

COMMON NAME
Scientific Name

Other Names: common terms or nicknames you may hear to describe this species

Habitat: environment where the fish is found (such as streams, rivers, small or large lakes, fast-flowing or still water, in or around vegetation, near shore, in clear water)

Range: geographic distribution, starting with the fish's overall range, followed by state-specific information

Food: what the fish eats most of the time (such as crustaceans, insects, fish, plankton)

Reproduction: timing of and behavior during the spawning period (dates and water temperatures, migration information, preferred spawning habitat, type of nest if applicable, colonial or solitary nester, parental care for eggs or fry)

Size: average length or range of length, average weight or range of weight

Records: State—the state record for this species, location and year; North American—the North American record for this species, location and year (based on the Fresh Water Fishing Hall of Fame)

Notes: Interesting natural history information. This can be unique behaviors, remarkable features, sporting and table quality, or details on migrations, seasonal patterns or population trends.

Description: long, stout body; rounded tail; long, continuous dorsal fin; large, toothy mouth; bony plates covering the head; brownish green back and sides with white belly; males have a large "eye" spot at the base of tail

Similar Species: Burbot (pg. 46), American Eel (pg. 50), Sea Lamprey (pg. 62)

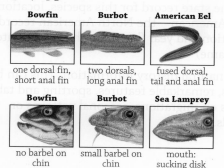

Bowfin	Burbot	American Eel
one dorsal fin, short anal fin	two dorsals, long anal fin	fused dorsal, tail and anal fin

Bowfin	Burbot	Sea Lamprey
no barbel on chin	small barbel on chin	mouth: sucking disk

BOWFIN
Amia calva

Amiidae

Other Names: dogfish, grindle, mudfish, cypress trout, lake lawyer, beaverfish

Habitat: deep waters associated with weedbeds in warm water lakes and rivers; feeds in shallow weeds

Range: Mississippi River east through St. Lawrence drainage, south from Texas to Florida; common throughout the Lower Peninsula of Michigan

Food: fish, crayfish

Reproduction: when water warms past 61 degrees in spring, male removes vegetation on sand or gravel bottom; one or more females deposit up to 5,000 eggs in nest; male guards until young reach about 4 inches in length

Average Size: 12 to 24 inches, 2 to 5 pounds

Records: State—14 pounds, Crooked Lake, Livingston County, 1981; North American—21 pounds, 8 ounces, Forest Lake, South Carolina, 1980

Notes: A voracious predator, the Bowfin prowls shallow weedbeds preying on anything that moves. Once thought detrimental to game fish populations, it is now considered an asset in controlling rough fish and stunted game fish. An air breather that tolerates oxygen-depletion, it can survive buried in mud for short periods during drought conditions. Not considered a game fish or sought by anglers.

33

Description: black to olive-green back; sides yellowish green; belly creamy to yellow; light bar on base of tail; barbels (dark at base) around mouth; adipose fin; scaleless skin; rounded tail

Similar Species: Brown Bullhead (pg. 36), Yellow Bullhead (pg. 38), Madtom/Stonecat (pg. 44), Flathead Catfish (pg. 42)

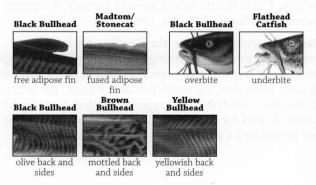

Black Bullhead	**Madtom/ Stonecat**	**Black Bullhead**	**Flathead Catfish**
free adipose fin	fused adipose fin	overbite	underbite

Black Bullhead	**Brown Bullhead**	**Yellow Bullhead**	
olive back and sides	mottled back and sides	yellowish back and sides	

BLACK BULLHEAD

Ameiurus melas

Ictaluridae

Other Names: common bullhead, horned pout

Habitat: shallow, slow-moving streams and backwaters; lakes and ponds--tolerates extremely turbid (cloudy) conditions

Range: southern Canada through the Great Lakes and the Mississippi River watershed into Mexico and the Southwest; common throughout Michigan

Food: a scavenging opportunist, feeds mostly on animal material (live or dead) but will eat plant matter

Reproduction: spawns from late April to early June; builds nest in shallow water with a muddy bottom; both sexes guard nest and eggs; male guards young to 1 inch in size

Average Size: 8 to 10 inches, 4 to 6 ounces

Records: State—3 pounds, 7 ounces, Magician Lake, Michigan, 1999; North American—8 pounds, 15 ounces, Sturgis Pond, Michigan, 1987 (not registered as a state record)

Notes: The Black Bullhead is the most abundant of the three bullhead species found in Michigan, and on average the smallest. However, in 1987 the North American record was set in Michigan with an 8-pound lunker. It is more common to find large numbers of stunted Black Bullheads overpopulating a pond than it is to catch one large enough to keep.

Description: yellowish brown upper body, with mottling on back and sides; barbels around mouth; adipose fin; scaleless skin; rounded tail; well-defined barbs on the pectoral spines

Similar Species: Black Bullhead (pg. 34), Yellow Bullhead (pg. 38), Madtom/Stonecat (pg. 44), Flathead Catfish (pg. 42)

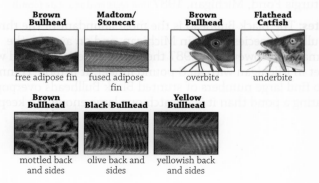

Brown Bullhead	Madtom/Stonecat	Brown Bullhead	Flathead Catfish
free adipose fin	fused adipose fin	overbite	underbite

Brown Bullhead	Black Bullhead	Yellow Bullhead
mottled back and sides	olive back and sides	yellowish back and sides

36

BROWN BULLHEAD

Ameiurus nebulosus

Ictaluridae

Other Names: marbled or speckled bullhead, red cat

Habitat: warm, weedy lakes and sluggish streams

Range: southern Canada through the Great Lakes down the eastern states to Florida, introduced in the West; most common in southern Michigan but represented throughout the state including the Upper Peninsula

Food: a scavenging opportunist; feeds mostly on insects, fish, fish eggs, snails and leeches but will eat plant matter

Reproduction: in early summer female and male build nest in shallow water with a sand or rocky bottom, often in cover offering shade; both sexes guard eggs and young

Average Size: 8 to 10 inches, 4 ounces to 2 pounds

Records: State—3 pounds, 9.9 ounces, Kalamazoo County, 1989; North American—6 pounds, 2 ounces, Pearl River, Mississippi, 1991

Notes: The Brown Bullhead is the least common bullhead in Michigan. It can tolerate very turbid (cloudy) water but prefers clean, weedy lakes with soft bottoms. Young bullheads are black, and in early summer are often seen swimming in a tight, swarming ball. An adult fish may be seen guarding this ball of fry. Not highly pursued by anglers, though its reddish meat is tasty and fine table fare.

Description: olive head and back; yellowish-green sides; white belly; barbels on lower jaw are pale green to white; scaleless skin, adipose fin, rounded tail

Similar Species: Brown Bullhead (pg. 36), Black Bullhead (pg. 34), Madtom/Stonecat (pg. 44), Flathead Catfish (pg. 42)

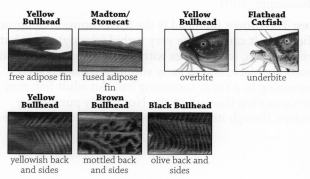

Yellow Bullhead	Madtom/ Stonecat	Yellow Bullhead	Flathead Catfish
free adipose fin	fused adipose fin	overbite	underbite

Yellow Bullhead	Brown Bullhead	Black Bullhead
yellowish back and sides	mottled back and sides	olive back and sides

YELLOW BULLHEAD

Ameiurus natalis

Other Names: white-whiskered bullhead, yellow cat

Habitat: warm, weedy lakes and sluggish streams

Range: southern Great Lakes through the eastern half of the U.S. to the Gulf and into Mexico; introduced in the West; common in Michigan's Lower Peninsula, rare in the Upper Peninsula

Food: a scavenging opportunist, feeds on insects, crayfish, snails, small fish and plant material

Reproduction: in late spring to early summer, male and female build nest in shallow water with some vegetation and a soft bottom; both sexes guard eggs and young

Average Size: 8 to 10 inches, 1 to 2 pounds

Records: State—3 pounds, 9.96 ounces, Lake Sixteen, Oakland County, 2002; North American—4 pounds, 15 ounces, Ogeechee River, Georgia, 2003

Notes: The Yellow Bullhead is common in the inland lakes of Michigan but not often taken from any of the Great Lakes. There are no records from Superior. Its cream-colored flesh has excellent flavor, but may become soft in summer. Bullheads feed by "taste," locating their food by following chemical trails through the water. This ability can be greatly diminished in polluted water, impairing their ability to find food. The Yellow Bullhead is less likely than other bullheads to overpopulate a lake and become stunted.

Description: gray to silver back and sides; white belly; black spots on sides; large fish lack spots and appear dark olive or slate; forked tail; adipose fin; long barbels around mouth

Similar Species: Blue Catfish, Flathead Catfish (pg.42), Bullheads (pg.34-39)

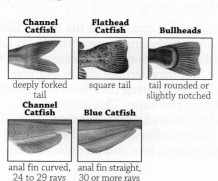

Channel Catfish	Flathead Catfish	Bullheads
deeply forked tail	square tail	tail rounded or slightly notched

Channel Catfish	Blue Catfish
anal fin curved, 24 to 29 rays	anal fin straight, 30 or more rays

CHANNEL CATFISH

Ictalurus punctatus

Ictaluridae

Other Names: spotted, speckled or silver catfish

Habitat: prefers clean, fast-moving streams with deep pools; stocked in many lakes; can tolerate turbid (cloudy) water

Range: southern Canada through the Midwest into Mexico and Florida; introduced through much of the U.S.; known from all Great Lake drainages in the southern half of Michigan

Food: insects, crustaceans, fish, some plant debris

Reproduction: in early summer male builds nest in dark, sheltered area such as an undercut bank or under logs; female deposits gelatinous egg mass; male guards eggs and young until the nest is deserted

Average Size: 12 to 20 inches, 3 to 4 pounds

Records: State—40 pounds, Houghton Lake, Roscommon County, 1964; North American—58 pounds, Santee Cooper Reservoir, South Carolina, 1964

Notes: The Channel Catfish is a highly regarded sport and food fish through much of the U.S. and around the world. It has been widely introduced in northern Asia and Europe. Though not commonly fished for in Michigan it provides great sport for the anglers who seek it out. Like other catfish, channels will feed both night and day, but serious catfish-ermen often pursue them at night. Very similar in appearance to the southern Blue Catfish.

Description: color variable, usually mottled yellow or brown; belly cream to yellow; adipose fin; chin barbels; lacks scales; head broad and flattened; tail squared; pronounced underbite

Similar Species: Channel Catfish (pg.40), Tadpole Madtom (pg.44), Bullheads (pp. 34-39)

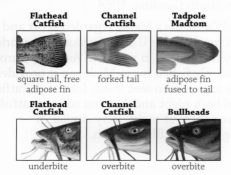

Flathead Catfish	Channel Catfish	Tadpole Madtom
square tail, free adipose fin	forked tail	adipose fin fused to tail

Flathead Catfish	Channel Catfish	Bullheads
underbite	overbite	overbite

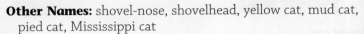

FLATHEAD CATFISH
Pylodictis olivaris

Ictaluridae

Other Names: shovel-nose, shovelhead, yellow cat, mud cat, pied cat, Mississippi cat

Habitat: deep pools of large rivers and impoundments

Range: the Mississippi River watershed and into Mexico; large rivers in the Southwest; a few rivers in the Lake Michigan drainage

Food: fish, crayfish

Reproduction: spawns when water is 72 to 80 degrees; male builds and defends nest in hollow log, undercut bank or other secluded area; female may lay more than 30,000 eggs, depending on her size and condition

Average Size: 20 to 30 inches, 10 to 20 pounds

Records: State—47 pounds, 8 ounces, Maple River, Ionia County, 1943; North American—123 pounds, Elk River Reservoir, Kansas

Notes: The Flathead Catfish is uncommon in Michigan and inhabits only a few large rivers in the Lake Michigan drainage. Despite its scarcity, a few dedicated anglers pursue it. A strong fighter with firm, white flesh. The Flathead is a large, typically solitary predator that feeds aggressively on live fish, often at night; rarely eats decaying animal matter. Often relates to logjams and deep pools. In some states it has been introduced in lakes to control stunted panfish.

STONECAT

TADPOLE MADTOM

Description: Tadpole Madtom—dark olive to brown; dark line on side; large, fleshy head; Stonecat—similar but lacks dark lateral stripe, and has protruding upper jaw; both species have adipose fin continuous with tail

Similar Species: Bullheads (pp. 34-39), Catfish (pp. 40-43)

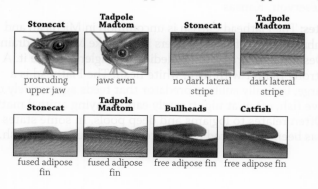

Stonecat	Tadpole Madtom	Stonecat	Tadpole Madtom
protruding upper jaw	jaws even	no dark lateral stripe	dark lateral stripe

Stonecat	Tadpole Madtom	Bullheads	Catfish
fused adipose fin	fused adipose fin	free adipose fin	free adipose fin

STONECAT *Noturus flavus*

Ictaluridae

TADPOLE MADTOM *Noturus gyrinus*

Other Name: willow cat

Habitat: weedy water near shore, under rocks in stream riffles

Range: eastern U.S.; both are native to southern Michigan and scattered areas of the Great Lakes

Food: small invertebrates, algae and other plant matter

Reproduction: spawn in late spring; not nest builders; female lays eggs under objects such as roots, rocks, logs or in abandoned crayfish burrows; nest guarded by one parent

Average Size: Tadpole Madtom—3 to 4 inches; Stonecat—4 to 6 inches

Records: none

Notes: Small, secretive fish most active at night. Both species have poison glands at the base of the dorsal and pectoral fins. Though not lethal, poison produces a painful burning sensation, reputed to bring even the hardiest anglers to their knees, if only for a short time. Stonecats, and to a lesser degree Tadpole Madtoms, are common baitfish in some states. They are favored by many veteran river Walleye anglers, who believe the tough little baitfish are superior to minnows and chubs. Indeed, more than a few high-stakes Walleye tournaments have been won by fishermen using "willow cats." Reportedly, damaging the "slime" coating (by rolling them in sand) to make handling easier will reduce their effectiveness as bait.

45

Description: eel-like body; mottled brown with creamy chin and belly; small barbel at each nostril opening, longer barbel on chin; rear part of dorsal similar in shape and just above anal fin

Similar Species: Bowfin (pg. 32), American Eel (pg. 50), Sea Lamprey (pg. 62)

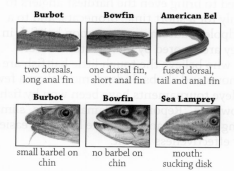

Burbot	Bowfin	American Eel
two dorsals, long anal fin	one dorsal fin, short anal fin	fused dorsal, tail and anal fin

Burbot	Bowfin	Sea Lamprey
small barbel on chin	no barbel on chin	mouth: sucking disk

BURBOT

Lota lota

Other Names: lawyer, eelpout, ling, cusk

Habitat: deep, cold, clear lakes and streams of the north

Range: northern North America into Siberia and across northern Europe; common in the Lake Superior, Michigan and Huron drainage, not found in southeast Michigan

Food: a voracious predator; primarily feeds on small fish but will attempt to eat virtually anything, including fish eggs, clams and crayfish

Reproduction: pairs to large groups spawn together in mid- to late winter, under the ice, over sand or gravel bottoms, usually in less than 15 feet of water; after spawning, thrashing adults scatter fertilized eggs; no nest is built and there is no parental care

Average Size: 20 inches, 2 to 8 pounds

Records: State—18 pounds, 4 ounces, St. Marys River, Chippewa County, 1980; North American—22 pounds, 8 ounces, Little Athapapuskow Lake, Manitoba, 1994

Notes: A freshwater member of the cod family, the Burbot is a coldwater fish, seldom found in fisheries where the water temperature routinely exceeds 69 degrees. It is popular with ice fishermen in some western states and Scandinavia but is not highly regarded in Michigan despite its firm, white, good-tasting flesh.

Description: humped back, dorsal fin extends from hump to near tail; back is gray with purple or bronze reflections, silver sides, white underbelly; only Michigan fish with lateral line running from head through the tail

Similar Species: White Bass (pg. 154)

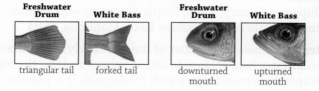

Freshwater Drum	White Bass	Freshwater Drum	White Bass
triangular tail	forked tail	downturned mouth	upturned mouth

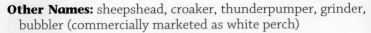

FRESHWATER DRUM

Sciaenidae

Aplodinotus grunniens

Other Names: sheepshead, croaker, thunderpumper, grinder, bubbler (commercially marketed as white perch)

Habitat: slow- to moderate-current areas of rivers and streams; shallow lakes, often with mud or sand bottoms; prefers turbid (cloudy) water

Range: Canada south through Midwest into eastern Mexico to Guatemala; in Michigan, rare inland, common in lakes St. Clair, Erie, and Michigan, and in Saginaw Bay

Food: small fish, insects, crayfish, clams, Zebra Mussels

Reproduction: in May and June after water temperature reaches about 66 degrees, schools of drum randomly lay eggs in open water near surface, over sand or gravel; no nest or parental care

Average Size: 10 to 14 inches, 2 to 5 pounds

Records: State—26 pounds, Muskegon Lake, Muskegon County, 1973; North American—54 pounds, 8 ounces, Nickajack Lake, Tennessee, 1972

Notes: The only freshwater member of the drum family, which is named for the grunting noise produced by males, primarily to attract females. The sound is produced by muscles rubbed along the swim bladder. The skull contains two large L-shaped earstones called otoliths. Not popular with sport anglers. Flaky white flesh is tasty but easily dries out when cooked due to its low oil content. Highly prized as food in the eastern Great Lakes basin often marketed as white perch.

Description: long, snake-like body with large mouth and pectoral fins; gill slits and continuous dorsal, tail and anal fin; dark brown on top with yellow sides and white belly

Similar Species: Sea Lamprey (pg. 62), Bowfin (pg. 32), Burbot (pg. 46)

American Eel	Bowfin	Burbot
fused dorsal, tail and anal fin	one dorsal fin, short anal fin	two dorsals, long anal fin

American Eel	Sea Lamprey
mouth: jaws	mouth: sucking disk

AMERICAN EEL

Anguilla rostrata

Other Names: common, Boston, Atlantic or freshwater eel

Habitat: soft bottoms of medium to large streams

Range: Atlantic Ocean, eastern and central North America, eastern Central America; uncommon but reported from all of Michigan's coastal drainages

Food: insects, crayfish, small fish

Reproduction: Michigan's only "catadromous" species, it spends most of its life in freshwater and spawns in the mid-North Atlantic Ocean in Sargasso Sea; female may lay up to 20 million eggs; adults die after spawning

Average Size: 24 to 36 inches, 1 to 3 pounds

Records: State—7 pounds, 7 ounces, Lake St. Clair, Macomb County, 1990; North American—8 pounds, 8 ounces, Cliff Pond, Massachusetts, 1992

Notes: Leaf-shaped larval eels drift with ocean currents for about a year. When they reach river mouths of North and Central America, they morph into small eels (elvers). Males remain in estuaries; females migrate upstream. At maturity (up to 20 years of age) adults return to Sargasso Sea. Not a popular food fish in Michigan but it is commercially fished along the East Coast. Most active at night.

51

Description: long, cylindrical profile; single dorsal fin located above anal fin; body is encased in hard, plate-like scales; snout twice as long as head; needle-sharp teeth on both jaws; olive to brown with dark spots along sides

Similar Species: Spotted Gar (pg. 54)

Longnose Gar	**Spotted Gar**
no spots on top of head or snout	spots on head and snout

LONGNOSE GAR
Lepisosteus osseus

Other Names: gar, garfish

Habitat: floodplain lakes and backwaters of large rivers

Range: central U.S. through the Mississippi drainage south into Mexico; in Michigan, common in all Lower Peninsula drainages

Food: minnows and small fish

Reproduction: large, green eggs are laid in weedy shallows of lakes or tributaries when water temperatures reach the high 60s; using a small disk on the snout, a newly hatched gar attaches itself to a nearby plant, rock or wood until its mouth and digestive tract forms enough to begin feeding

Average Size: 24 to 36 inches, 2 to 5 pounds

Records: State—18 pounds, Williamsville Lake, Livingston County, 1995; North American—50 pounds, 5 ounces, Trinity River, Texas, 1954

Notes: The Longnose Gar can breathe air at the surface, thanks to a modified swim bladder; this allows it to survive in hot shallows lacking enough oxygen for most other fish. Prefers warm, deep water but will school near the surface. An efficient predator that helps control rough fish populations, it stalks small fish, then makes a quick, sideways slash to capture them. May grow to lengths of five feet. With the increased siltation of many southern Michigan streams and lakes, this hardy fish has become an asset in controlling large rough fish populations.

Description: cylindrical body; long, toothy jaws; hard, armor-like scales; dorsal and anal fins aligned near tail; olive brown with spots covering head, body and fins; snout is slightly longer than the head

Similar Species: Longnose Gar (pg. 52)

Longnose Gar	Spotted Gar
no spots on top of head or snout	spots on head and snout

SPOTTED GAR

Lepisosteus oculatus

Common Names: speckled gar

Habitat: quiet, clear, weedy water in streams and lakes

Range: southern Great Lakes basin southeast to Florida; southwestern corner of Michigan in Lake Michigan basin

Food: minnows, small fish

Reproduction: spawns from May through June in quiet backwaters

Size: 12 to 24 inches, 1 to 2 pounds

Records: State—none; North American—28 pounds, 8 ounces, Lake Seminole, Florida, 1987

Notes: The Spotted Gar is uncommon in Michigan and is on the decline. It requires cleaner, more weedy water than other gars. Increased silt loads from runoff in Michigan streams have reduced the amount of suitable habitat. Like other gars, the Spotted Gar can gulp air and use its specialized swim bladder as a modified lung to breathe. The gars are prized as food in the South but have little respect with anglers in the North.

Description: silvery with blue to blue-green metallic shine on back with silver sides and white belly; faint dark stripes along sides; dark spot behind the gill, directly above the pectoral fin; large mouth with protruding lower jaw

Similar Species: Gizzard Shad (pg. 58), Mooneye (pg. 76)

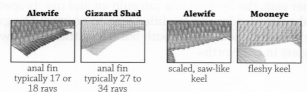

Alewife	Gizzard Shad	Alewife	Mooneye
anal fin typically 17 or 18 rays	anal fin typically 27 to 34 rays	scaled, saw-like keel	fleshy keel

ALEWIFE
Alosa pseudoharengus

Clupeidae

Other Names: ellwife, sawbelly, shad or golden shad, big-eyed herring, river herring

Habitat: open water of the Great Lakes and a few inland lakes; found in Michigan's lakes Superior, Michigan and Huron

Range: Atlantic Ocean from Labrador to Florida; St. Lawrence River drainage and the Great Lakes

Food: zooplankton, filamentous algae

Reproduction: in the Great Lakes, spawning takes place in open water of bays and along protected shorelines during early summer

Average Size: 4 to 8 inches

Records: none

Notes: This Atlantic herring reached the upper Great Lakes in 1931, Lake Huron in 1933, Lake Michigan in 1949 and Lake Superior in 1953. With the depletion of large predators by the Sea Lamprey the Alewife population had exploded in Lakes Michigan and Huron by the late 1950's to early 1960's. There is a much smaller population of Alewives in Lake Superior. Not well adapted to freshwater lakes, the Alewife is subject to frequent large summerkills. The Alewife is the main forage for the salmon and Lake Trout in the Great Lakes and is used commercially for animal food.

57

Description: deep body; silvery blue back with white sides and belly; small mouth; last rays of dorsal fin form a long thread; younger fish have a dark spot behind the gill flap

Similar Species: Alewife (pg. 56), Mooneye (pg. 76)

Gizzard Shad	Alewife	Gizzard Shad	Mooneye
anal fin typically 27 to 34 rays	anal fin typically 17 or 18 rays	scaled, saw-like keel	fleshy keel

GIZZARD SHAD

Dorosoma cepedianum

Other Names: hickory, mud or jack shad, skipjack

Habitat: large rivers, reservoirs, lakes, swamps; brackish and saline waters in coastal areas

Range: St. Lawrence River and Great Lakes, Mississippi, Atlantic and Gulf Slope drainages from Quebec to Mexico, south to central Florida; in Michigan, Lake Michigan, Huron and Erie drainages

Food: herbivorous filter feeder

Reproduction: spawning takes place in tributary streams and along lakeshores in early summer; eggs and milt are released in schools, without regard for individual mates

Average Size: 6 to 8 inches, 1 to 8 ounces

Records: State—4 pounds, 2 ounces, Lake St. Clair, St. Clair County, 1996; North American—4 pounds, 12 ounces; Lake Oahe, South Dakota, 2006

Notes: The Gizzard Shad is a widespread, prolific fish that is best known as forage for popular game fish. At times it can become over-abundant and experience large die-offs. The name "gizzard" refers to its long, convoluted intestine, which is often packed with sand. Though Gizzard Shad are a management problem at times they form a valuable link in turning plankton into usable forage for large predators. Occasionally larger Gizzard Shad are caught with hook and line, but they have little food value.

CHESTNUT LAMPREY

Description: eel-like body with round, sucking-disk mouth and seven paired gill openings; dorsal fin is long, extending to the tail; no paired fins.

Similar Species: Sea Lamprey (pg. 62), Bowfin (pg. 32), Burbot (pg. 46), American Eel (pg. 50)

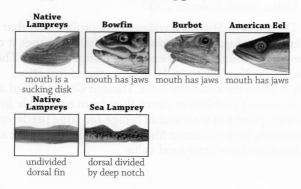

Native Lampreys	Bowfin	Burbot	American Eel
mouth is a sucking disk	mouth has jaws	mouth has jaws	mouth has jaws

Native Lampreys	Sea Lamprey
undivided dorsal fin	dorsal divided by deep notch

NATIVE LAMPREYS

Ichthyomyzon, Lampetra

Other Names: Silver, Chestnut, Northern Brook and American Brook Lamprey

Habitat: juveniles live in the quiet pools of streams and rivers; adults may move into some lakes

Range: freshwater of eastern North America; the Silver, Northern and American Brook Lampreys are distributed throughout Michigan. The Chestnut Lamprey is only found in the Lower Peninsula

Food: juvenile lampreys are filter feeders in stream bottoms; adults are either parasitic on fish or do not feed

Reproduction: adults build nest in the gravel of streambeds, typically after water temperatures reach about 55 degrees, then die shortly after spawning

Average Size: 6 to 12 inches

Records: none

Notes: Modern lampreys are relatives to the oldest vertebrates found on earth with fossil records dating back 500 million years. There are four lampreys native to Michigan. The Silver and Chestnut Lampreys are parasitic on fish in the adult form, leaving small round wounds on their prey. The Northern and American Brook lampreys are non-parasitic and do not feed as adults. All are secretive stream dwellers, with little impact on native fish populations.

Description: eel-like body; round, sucking-disk mouth; seven paired gill openings; dorsal fin extends to the tail and is divided into two sections by a deep notch; no paired fins

Similar Species: Native Lampreys (pg. 60), Bowfin (pg. 32), Burbot (pg. 40), American Eel (pg. 50),

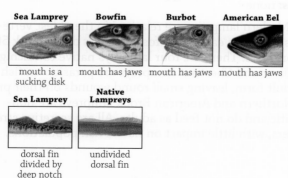

Sea Lamprey	Bowfin	Burbot	American Eel
mouth is a sucking disk	mouth has jaws	mouth has jaws	mouth has jaws

Sea Lamprey	Native Lampreys
dorsal fin divided by deep notch	undivided dorsal fin

SEA LAMPREY

Petromyzon marinus

Petromyzontidae

Other Names: landlocked or lake lamprey

Habitat: juveniles live in quiet pools of freshwater streams; adults are free-swimming in lakes or oceans

Range: Atlantic Ocean from Greenland to Florida, Norway to the Mediterranean; the Great Lakes; in Michigan, in lakes Superior, Michigan and Huron and some tributaries

Food: juvenile form is a filter feeder in the bottom of streams; adult is parasitic on fish, attaching itself using disk-shaped sucker mouth and sharp teeth, then using its sharp tongue to rasp through the fish's scales and skin to feed on blood and bodily fluids; many "host" fish die

Reproduction: adults build nest in the gravel of a clear stream, then die shortly after spawning; young remain in stream several years before returning to the lake as adults

Average Size: 12 to 24 inches

Records: none

Notes: Native to the Atlantic Ocean, the Sea Lamprey entered the Great Lakes via the St. Lawrence Seaway. It was initially blocked by Niagara Falls, but when the Welland Canal allowed it to bypass the falls, it entered the upper Great Lakes. The first was recorded from Lake Superior in 1936. Two years later one was found in Lake Michigan. Soon after, the Lake Trout and Whitefish populations began to decline. With the use of traps and chemicals, the Sea Lamprey population is now under partial control.

63

BIGHEAD CARP

Description: large body; upturned mouth without barbels; low-set eyes; small scales on body, none on the head

Similar Species: Common Carp (pg. 66), Black Buffalo (pg. 120)

Asian Carp	Common Carp	Black Buffalo
upturned mouth lacks barbels; eyes low on head	down-turned mouth with barbels	eyes set high on head

ASIAN CARP

Cyprinidae

bighead, black, grass and silver carp
Ctenopharyngodon, Hypophthalmichthys

Other Names: carp, flyers, jumpers

Habitat: large, warm rivers and connected lakes

Range: native to Asia, introduced in other parts of the world; in Michigan, a few streams and possibly the Great Lakes

Food: aquatic vegetation, floating plankton

Reproduction: spawns from late spring to early summer in warm, flowing water

Average Size: 16 to 22 inches, 5 to 50 pounds

Records: Grass Carp, North American—78 pounds, 12 ounces, Flint River, Georgia, 2003; Bighead Carp, North American—90 pounds, Kirby Lake, Texas, 2000

Notes: Four species of Asian Carp were introduced into the U.S. to control algae in southern aquaculture ponds and then escaped to the Mississippi River. The Black and Grass Carp are not threatening Michigan waters at this time, but the Silver and Bighead Carp—voracious plankton feeders with the potential to disrupt the entire food web—pose a serious risk. The Silver Carp, and to a lesser degree the Bighead, make high leaps from the water when frightened by boats, occasionally injuring boaters.

65

Description: two pairs of barbels near round, extendable mouth; brassy yellow to golden brown or dark-olive sides; white belly; some red on tail and anal fin; each scale has a dark spot at the base and a dark margin

Similar Species: Asian Carp (pg. 64), Black Buffalo (pg. 120), Quillback (pg. 122)

Common Carp	Asian Carp	Black Buffalo	Quillback
down-turned mouth with barbels, eyes high on head	upturned mouth lacks barbels, eyes low on head	lacks barbels	lacks barbels

COMMON CARP

Cyprinus carpio

Other Names: German, European, mirror or leather carp, buglemouth

Habitat: warm, shallow, quiet, well-vegetated waters of both streams and lakes

Range: native to Asia, widely introduced elsewhere; in Michigan, common in the southeast half of the Lower Peninsula, absent or rare in the northeast, rare in the U.P.

Food: prefers insects, crustaceans and mollusks but at times eats algae and other plants

Reproduction: spawns from late spring to early summer in very shallow water at stream and lake edges; adults are easily seen due to energetic splashing along shore

Average Size: 16 to 18 inches, 5 to 20 pounds

Records: State—61 pounds, 8 ounces, Wolf Lake, Jackson County, 1974 (not registered as a North American record); North American—57 pounds, 13 ounces, Tidal Basin, Washington D.C., 1983

Notes: The Common Carp is despised by many anglers, yet provides sport and food for millions worldwide. A fast-growing Asian minnow, it was introduced into Europe in the twelfth century and North America in the 1870s. It has become a large part of the fish biomass in the some waters. On the negative side, Common Carp uproot aquatic plants and increase turbidity in shallow lakes, causing a decline in waterfowl and native fish populations. Because of this it is sometimes the target of eradication efforts.

67

Description: gray to olive brown, often with a dark stripe on side and black spot at the base of tail; red spot behind eye; breeding males develop horn-like tubercles on the head

Similar Species: Fathead Minnow (pg. 72), Creek Chub

Hornyhead Chub

down-turned mouth extends to eye

Fathead Minnow

upturned mouth does not extend to eye

Creek Chub

mouth extends to middle of eye

HORNYHEAD CHUB

Nocomis biguttatus

Cyprinidae

Other Names: redtail, horned or river chub

Habitat: small to medium-size streams; occasionally found in lakes near stream mouths

Range: northern Midwest through the Great Lakes region; common in Michigan's Lower Peninsula and the western Upper Peninsula

Food: small aquatic invertebrates, zooplankton

Reproduction: in late spring male excavates a 1- to 3-foot diameter pit in gravelly stream riffle, then fills it with small stones (carried in by mouth), creating a 6- to 8-inch-high mound; females lay eggs on the mound; male covers fertilized eggs with gravel; other species such as Common Shiner may also use the mound for spawning, and some research suggests the two males cooperate to defend the nest

Average Size: 4 to 12 inches

Records: none

Notes: Michigan's six chubs are our largest native minnows. The Creek and Hornyhead grow to a foot long and can be caught with hook and line. The Hornyhead is a common bait minnow, often called Redtail Chub. In situations such as fall Walleye fishing it is the preferred bait, outfishing other species such as Common Shiner by a wide margin. Due to high demand, anglers sometimes pay $8 or more per dozen, making it costlier per pound than lobster.

Description: moderately dark back; two broad lateral bands on tan background; in breeding males, the tan turns orange and the belly becomes bright red or orange; blunt nose

Similar Species: Southern Redbelly Dace, Finescale Dace

Northern Redbelly Dace	**Southern Redbelly Dace**	**Northern Redbelly Dace**	**Finescale Dace**
curved mouth, lower jaw slightly ahead of upper	straight mouth, upper jaw slightly ahead of the lower	two dark lateral stripes	single dark lateral stripe

NORTHERN REDBELLY DACE

Phoxinus eos

Cyprinidae

Other Names: redbelly, leatherback, yellow-belly dace

Habitat: small streams and bog lakes

Range: Northwest Territories to Hudson Bay, northeastern U.S. and eastern Canada; common in most of Michigan, but absent from the southern border area

Food: bottom feeder that primarily eats plant material

Reproduction: from May to early August, a single female accompanied by several males will dart among masses of filamentous algae, laying 5 to 30 non-adhesive eggs at a time; males fertilize the eggs, which hatch in 8 to 10 days with no parental care

Average Size: 2 to 3 inches

Records: none

Notes: There are seven species of minnows in Michigan that are referred to as dace. These small fish live in a variety of habitats. The Northern Redbelly Dace is a hardy fish often found in the acid water of bog-stained lakes and beaver ponds; it also lives in small streams. Breeding males are one of Michigan's brightest colored fish and surpass many aquarium fish in beauty. Northern Redbelly Dace often hybridize with other species and sometimes form all-female populations.

Description: olive back, golden yellow sides and white belly; dark lateral line widens to spot at base of tail; rounded snout and fins; no scales on head; dark blotch on dorsal fin

Similar Species: Hornyhead Chub (pg. 68), Creek Chub

Fathead Minnow	Hornyhead Chub	Fathead Minnow	Creek Chub
upturned mouth does not extend to eye	down-turned mouth extends to eye	anal fin has 7 rays	anal fin has 8 rays

FATHEAD MINNOW

Pemephales promelas

Other Names: fathead, blackhead, tuffy, mudminnow

Habitat: streams, ponds and lakes, particularly shallow, weedy or turbid (cloudy) areas lacking predators

Range: east of the Rocky Mountains in the U.S. and Canada; statewide in Michigan

Food: primarily herbivorous but will eat insects and copepods

Reproduction: from the time water temperatures reach 60 degrees in spring through August, male prepares nest under rocks and sticks; female enters, turns upside down and lays adhesive eggs on the overhead object; after the female leaves, the male fertilizes the eggs, which it then guards, fans with its fins and massages with a special, mucus-like pad on its back

Average Size: 3 to 4 inches

Records: none

Notes: Minnows are small fish, not the young of larger species. The Fathead is one of our most numerous and widespread fish, commonly used as bait. It is hardy and withstands extremely low oxygen levels—both in the wild and in bait buckets. Prior to spawning, the male develops a dark coloration, breeding tubercles on its head that resemble small horns, and a mucus-like patch on its back; during this phase, anglers report having better luck when using female Fatheads, perhaps due to their color or differing scent.

Description: silver body with dark green back, often with a dark body stripe; breeding males have bluish heads and rosy pink on body and fins

Similar Species: Golden Shiner, Creek Chub

Common Shiner	Golden Shiner	Common Shiner	Creek Chub
8 to 10 rays on anal fin (usually 9)	11 to 15 rays on anal fin	mouth barely extends to eye, which is large in relation to head	mouth extends almost to middle of eye, which is small in relation to head

COMMON SHINER

Notropis cornutus

Other Names: common, eastern, creek or redfin shiner

Habitat: lakes, rivers and streams; most common in the pools of streams and small rivers

Range: Midwest through eastern U.S. and Canada; widespread in Michigan, in both Upper and Lower Peninsula

Food: small insects, algae and zooplankton

Reproduction: beginning in late May, male prepares nest of small stones and gravel at the head of a stream riffle (sometimes using the nest of a Creek Chub or Hornyhead Chub); other males are chased away, but females are courted with great flourish; it is generally thought that after spawning, both male and female abandon the nest, but research has documented male Common Shiners and Hornyhead Chubs cooperating to defend a nest

Average Size: 4 to 12 inches

Records: none

Notes: Not all shiners are as flashy as the name indicates. Some are dull-colored and show almost no silver on the sides. The Common Shiner is one of the larger native Michigan minnows, occasionally reaching 12 inches in length. It has now replaced the Golden Shiner as the common bait shiner, though it seems somewhat less hardy on the hook. Large Common Shiners can be caught on dry flies and are occasionally eaten; though not as meaty as panfish, they are every bit as tenacious when hooked.

75

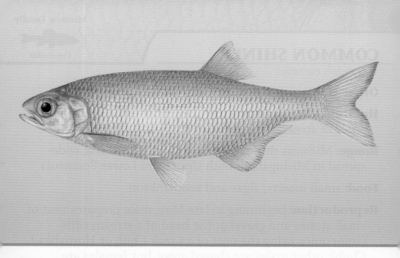

Description: silver with olive back; large scales on body but none on the head; large, white eye more than one third the width of head; thin body with a sharp scale-less keel between pelvic and anal fins

Similar Species: Gizzard Shad (pg. 58)

Mooneye	Gizzard Shad

fleshy keel | scaled, saw-like keel

MOONEYE

Hiodon tergisus

Other Names: white shad, slicker, toothed herring, river whitefish

Habitat: clear, quiet waters of large lakes and the backwaters of large streams

Range: Hudson Bay drainage south through the Ohio and Mississippi drainage to Tennessee; once common in Michigan but now found only in Lake St. Clair and the St. Clair River

Food: insects, small fish, crayfish, snails

Reproduction: spawning takes place in clear backwaters and over rocks in swift-water areas when water temperatures reach the mid-50s; a single female may release up to 20,000 gelatin-covered eggs

Average Size: 12 inches, 12 to 16 ounces

Records: State—1 pound, 11 ounces, Lake St. Clair, St. Clair County, 1995; North American—1 pound, 12 ounces; Lake Poygan, Wisconsin, 2000

Notes: The Mooneye is a flashy fish that jumps repeatedly when hooked. However, it is bony, with little meat except along the back, and is not a good table fish. It commonly feeds on insects at or near the surface in slack waters of large lakes and rivers. Because it requires clean, clear water it is becoming less common due to the siltation of many streams. Though small, it is related to the South American Arapaima, the world's largest scaled freshwater fish.

IOWA DARTER

JOHNNY
DARTER

Description: Iowa Darter—brown back with faint blotches; sides have 9 to 12 vertical bars; dark spot under eye; bars become more pronounced and colors brighter on breeding males; Johnny Darter—tan to olive back and upper sides with dark blotches and speckling; sides tan to golden with X, Y and W patterns; breeding males dark with black bars

Species: Iowa Darter; Johnny Darter

Iowa Darter	Johnny Darter
blotches or bars on sides	X, Y and W markings on sides

IOWA DARTER *Etheostoma exile*
JOHNNY DARTER *Etheostoma nigrum*

Other Names: red-sided, yellowbelly or weed darter

Habitat: Iowa Darters inhabit slow-flowing streams and lakes that have some vegetation or an algae mat; Johnny Darters are found in most rivers, streams and lakes

Range: Rocky Mountains east across Canada and the U.S. through the Great Lakes region; some species of darter can be found in most of the streams in Michigan; the Iowa Darter is common in most lakes throughout Michigan

Food: waterfleas, insect larvae

Reproduction: in May and June, males migrate to shorelines to establish breeding areas; females move from territory to territory, spawning with several males; each sequence produces 7 to 10 eggs, which sink and attach to the bottom

Average Size: 2 to 4 inches

Records: none

Notes: Relatives of Yellow Perch and Walleye, darters are primarily stream fish that live among rocks in fast current. Small swim bladders allow them to sink rapidly to bottom after making a quick "dart," thus avoiding being swept away by the current. The Johnny is the most common, found in most lakes, streams and rivers statewide. The Iowa Darter is a lake species that inhabits weedy shorelines. Hard to see when still, but easy to spot when making a quick dart to a new resting place, where they perch on pectoral fins. Iowa Darters make fine aquarium fish but require live food.

Description: slender body; gray to dark silver or yellowish brown with dark blotches on sides; black spots on spiny dorsal fin; may exhibit some white on lower margin of tail, but lacks prominent white spot found on Walleye

Similar Species: Walleye (pg. 82)

Sauger	Walleye	Sauger	Walleye
no white spot on tail	white spot on bottom of tail	spiny dorsal fin is spotted, lacks dark blotch on rear base	spiny dorsal fin lacks spots, has large dark spot on rear base

SAUGER
Sander canadenses

Other Names: sand pike, spotfin pike, river pike, jackfish, jack salmon

Habitat: large lakes and rivers

Range: large lakes in southern Canada, northern U.S. and the larger reaches of the Mississippi, Missouri, Ohio and Tennessee River drainages; in Michigan, historically common in Lake Erie and Saginaw Bay; present but less common in lakes Michigan, Huron and Superior; in the last 20 years found only in the St. Clair River and Lake St. Clair

Food: small fish, aquatic insects, crayfish

Reproduction: spawns in April and May as water approaches 50 degrees; adults move into the shallow waters of tributaries and headwaters to randomly deposit eggs over gravel beds

Average Size: 12 to 13 inches, 8 ounces to 2 pounds

Records: State—6 pounds, 8 ounces, Torch Lake, Houghton County, 1976; North American—8 pounds, 12 ounces, Lake Sakakawea, North Dakota, 1971

Notes: Though the Sauger is the Walleye's smaller cousin it is a big-water fish primarily found in large lakes and rivers. Saugers were never common in Michigan but have declined greatly in the past twenty years. The reasons for the decline are not clear. Saugers are still common in other parts of the Great Lakes region and the upper Mississippi River.

Description: long, round body; dark silver or golden to dark olive brown in color; spines in both first dorsal and anal fin; sharp canine teeth; dark spot at base of the three last spines in the dorsal fin; white spot on bottom lobe of tail

Similar Species: Sauger (pg. 80)

Walleye	Sauger	Walleye	Sauger

| white spot on bottom of tail | no white spot on tail | spiny dorsal fin lacks spots, has large dark spot on rear base | spiny dorsal fin is spotted, lacks dark blotch on rear base |

WALLEYE
Sander vitreus

Other Names: marble-eyes, 'eye, walter, walleyed pike, jack, jackfish, pickerel

Habitat: lakes and streams, abundant in very large lakes

Range: originally the northern states and Canada, now widely stocked in the U.S.; common in all but the south-western part of Michigan

Food: mainly small fish, but also eats insects, crayfish, leeches and other small prey as opportunity permits

Reproduction: spawning takes place in tributary streams or rocky lake shoals when spring water temperatures reach 45 to 50 degrees; no parental care

Average Size: 14 to 17 inches, 1 to 3 pounds

Records: State—17 pounds 3 ounces, Pine River, Manistee County, 1951; North American—21 pounds, 11 ounces, Greer's Ferry Lake, Arkansas, 1982

Notes: Revered by anglers. Not a spectacular fighter, but ranks high in table quality. One- to 3-pound fish are excellent eating; breaking the 10-pound mark is a milestone in most fishing careers. A reflective layer of pigment in the eye, called *tapetum lucidum*, allows it to see well in low-light conditions, giving it an advantage over prey species such as Yellow Perch, which have poorer night vision or cannot quickly adapt to reduced light levels. As a result, Walleyes (particularly in clear lakes) are often most active at dusk, dawn, night and in light-reducing conditions such as waves or heavy cloud cover.

Description: 6 to 9 dark, vertical bars on bright yellowish green to orange background; long dorsal fin with two distinct lobes; lower fins have a yellow to orange tinge

Similar Species: Trout-perch (pg. 158), Walleye (pg. 82)

Yellow Perch	Trout-perch	Yellow Perch	Walleye
no adipose fin	adipose fin	lacks promi- nent white spot on tail	prominent white spot on tail

YELLOW PERCH

Perca flavescens

Other Names: ringed, striped or jack perch, green hornet

Habitat: lakes and streams preferring clear open water

Range: widely introduced throughout northern U.S. and southern Canada; common throughout Michigan

Food: small fish, insects, snails, leeches and crayfish

Reproduction: spawns at night in shallow, weedy areas after ice-out when water warms to 45 degrees; female drapes gelatinous ribbons of eggs over submerged vegetation

Average Size: 8 to 11 inches, 6 to 10 ounces

Records: State—3 pounds, 12 ounces, Lake Independence, Marquette County, 1947; North American—4 pounds, 3 ounces, Bordentown, New Jersey, 1865

Notes: Yellow Perch are very common, in Michigan and possibly the most important food and sport fish in the state. Perch congregate in large schools and are active throughout the year providing endless hours of enjoyment for anglers. Yellow Perch reproduction in the Great Lakes seems to be adversely effected by high Alewife populations. The perch population quickly recovers in years that the Alewife population crashes.

Description: olive-green to yellow-brown with wavy bars on the sides; distinct dark teardrop below the eye

Similar Species: Northern Pike (pg. 90), Muskellunge (pg. 88)

Grass Pickerel	Northern Pike	Grass Pickerel	Northern Pike
gill cover fully scaled	lower half of gill cover unscaled	dark teardrop under the eye	lacks dark teardrop

Grass Pickerel	Muskellunge
rounded tail	pointed tail

GRASS PICKEREL

Esox americanus

Common Names: grass or mud pike, mud or little pickerel

Habitat: shallow, weedy lakes and sluggish streams

Range: eastern one-third of the U.S. from the Great Lakes basin to Maine, south to Florida; common in the southern half of Michigan's Lower Peninsula

Food: small fish, aquatic insects

Reproduction: spawning takes place in April and May just as the ice goes out; eggs are laid in shallow weedbeds

Size: 12 inches

Records: State—no record; North American—1 pound, Dewart Lake, Indiana, 1990

Notes: The Grass Pickerel is very common in some southern Michigan lakes but is too small to be either a panfish or a game fish. Anglers catching Grass Pickerel often think they are small Northern Pike and return them to the water to "grow up." It is unclear what relationship there is between Grass Pickerel and Northern Pike. In some lakes they coexist, while in others there is just one of the two.

MUSKELLUNGE

TIGER MUSKIE

Description: torpedo-shaped body; dorsal fin near tail; sides typically silver to silver-green with dark spots or bars on light background; pointed lobes on tail; lower half of gill cover has no scales

Similar Species: Northern Pike (pg. 90), Tiger Muskie (pg. 88)

Muskellunge	Northern Pike	Muskellunge	Northern Pike
dark marks on light background	light marks on dark background	6 or more pores on each side under the jaw	5 or fewer pores each side under the jaw

Muskellunge	Northern Pike	Tiger Muskie
pointed tail	rounded tail	rounded tail

MUSKELLUNGE
Esox masquinongy

Other Names: musky, muskie, 'ski, lunge

Habitat: large, clear lakes with extensive weedbeds; also medium to large rivers with slow currents and deep pools

Range: the Great Lakes basin east to Maine, south through the Ohio River drainage to Tennessee; uncommon to rare in Michigan, the Lake St. Clair area in the southeast, the northeast corner of the Lower Peninsula and a few lakes and streams in the U.P.

Food: small fish, occasionally muskrats, ducklings

Reproduction: spawns mid-April to May at 50- to 60-degree water temperatures; eggs are laid in dead vegetation in tributaries, or in shallow bays with muck bottoms; male and female swim side by side for several hundred yards, depositing fertilized eggs

Average Size: 30 to 42 inches, 10 to 20 pounds

Records: State—49 pounds, 12 ounces, Thornapple Lake, Barry County, 2000; North American—69 pounds, 11 ounces, Chippewa Flowage, Wisconsin, 1949

Notes: This large predator resides primarily in the Great Lakes but is rare to uncommon in Michigan. Prefers shallow, weedy lakes and slow-moving streams but occasionally show up in deep, rocky lakes with few weedbeds. Readily hybridizes with Northern Pike to produce Tiger Muskies. In 1919, a record 51-pound Tiger was caught in Gogebic County.

89

Description: long body with dorsal fin near tail; head is long and flattened in front, forming a duck-like snout; dark green back, light green sides with bean-shaped light spots; Silver Pike are a rare, silver colored race of Northern Pike

Similar Species: Muskellunge (pg. 88), Tiger Muskie (pg. 88)

Northern Pike	Muskellunge	Tiger Muskie
light spots on dark background	dark marks on light background	dark marks on light background

Northern Pike	Muskellunge	Northern Pike	Muskellunge
rounded tail	pointed tail	five or fewer pores on underside of jaw	6 or more pores on each side under the jaw

NORTHERN PIKE

Esox lucius

Esocidae

Other Names: pickerel, jack, gator, hammerhandle, snot rocket

Habitat: lakes, ponds, streams and rivers; often found near weeds; small pike tolerate water temperatures up to 70 degrees but larger fish prefer cooler water, 55 degrees or less

Range: northern Europe, Asia and North America; common throughout Michigan and in the shallows of all three Great Lakes

Food: small fish, occasionally frogs, crayfish

Reproduction: late March to early April in tributaries and marshes at 34- to 40-degree water temperatures; attended by 1 to 3 males, female deposits eggs in shallow vegetation

Average Size: 18 to 24 inches, 2 to 5 pounds

Records: State—39 pounds, Dodge Lake, Schoolcraft County, 1961; North American—46 pounds, 2 ounces, Sacandaga Reservoir, New York, 1940

Notes: This large, fast predator is one of the most widespread freshwater fish in the world and a prime sportfish throughout its range. Its long, tube-shaped body and intramuscular bones are adaptations for quick bursts of speed in pursuit of prey. Northern Pike have firm, white flesh that can become fishy tasting if allowed contact with the pike's outer slime. They willingly hit a variety of live and artificial baits, and fight hard when hooked. The Tiger Muskellunge is a Northern Pike-Muskellunge hybrid

Description: back is olive, blue-gray to black with wormlike markings; sides are bronze to olive with red spots tinged light brown; lower fins red-orange with white leading edge; tail squared or slightly forked

Similar Species: Brown Trout (pg. 94), Rainbow Trout (pg. 98), Lake Trout (pg. 96), Splake

Brook Trout	Brown Trout	Rainbow Trout	Lake Trout
worm-like markings, red spots	large dark spots, small red dots	pink stripe on silver body	sides lack red spots

Brook Trout	Lake Trout	Splake
tail square to slightly forked	tail deeply forked	tail moderately forked

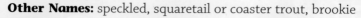

BROOK TROUT
Salvelinus fontinalis

Other Names: speckled, squaretail or coaster trout, brookie

Habitat: cool, clear streams and small lakes with sand or gravel bottoms and moderate vegetation; coastal Lake Superior; prefers water temperatures of 50 to 60 degrees

Range: Great Lakes region north to Labrador, south through the Appalachians to Georgia; introduced into the western U.S., Canada, Europe and South America; found throughout Michigan, but are most common in the eastern half of the Lower Peninsula and all of the Upper Peninsula

Food: insects, small fish, leeches, crustaceans

Reproduction: spawns in late fall at 40- to 49-degree water temperatures on gravel bars in stream riffles and in lakes where springs aerate eggs; female builds 4- to 12-inch-deep nest (male may guard during construction) in gravel, then buries fertilized eggs, which hatch in 50 to 150 days

Average Size: 8 to 10 inches, 8 ounces

Records: State—9 pounds, 8 ounces, Clear Lake, 1996; North American—14 pounds, 8 ounces, Nipigon River, Ontario, 1916

Notes: The state fish of Michigan, the Brook Trout requires cold, clear water, no warmer than the mid 50s, and most commonly inhabits the headwaters of spring-fed streams. Occurs naturally in some cold, deep lakes and is stocked in others. Large Brook Trout called "coasters" occur in Lake Superior near the mouth of tributary streams.

BROWN TROUT

TIGER TROUT

Description: golden-brown to olive back and sides; large dark spots on sides, dorsal fin and sometimes upper lobe of tail; red spots with light halos scattered along sides

Similar Species: Rainbow Trout (pg. 98), Lake Trout (pg. 96), Brook Trout (pg. 92), Tiger Trout

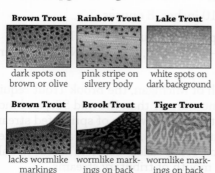

Brown Trout	Rainbow Trout	Lake Trout
dark spots on brown or olive	pink stripe on silvery body	white spots on dark background

Brown Trout	Brook Trout	Tiger Trout
lacks wormlike markings	wormlike markings on back	wormlike markings on back and sides

BROWN TROUT
Salmo trutta

Other Names: German brown, Loch Leven or spotted trout

Habitat: open ocean near its spawning streams and clear, cold, gravel-bottomed streams; shallow areas of Lake Superior

Range: native to Europe from the Mediterranean to Arctic Norway and Siberia, introduced worldwide; established in cold streams throughout Michigan and Lake Superior (absent from the "thumb"), stocked in Lake Michigan

Food: insects, crayfish, small fish

Reproduction: spawns October through December in stream headwaters and tributaries; stream mouths are used when migration is blocked; female fans out saucer-shaped nest, which male guards until spawning; female covers eggs

Average Size: 11 to 20 inches, 2 to 6 pounds

Records: State—34 pounds, 10 ounces, Lake Michigan, Manistee County, 2000; North American—40 pounds, 4 ounces, Little Red River, Arkansas, 1992

Notes: This European trout was brought to North America in 1883 and was well established in the Great Lakes region by the early 1900s. Brown Trout reproduce naturally in many Michigan streams, however the sport fishery is dependent on continual stocking. Brook and Brown Trout occasionally cross, producing a sterile hybrid called the Tiger Trout. Brown Trout are secretive, hard-to-catch fish that often feed at night; they are highly prized by fly fishermen throughout the world.

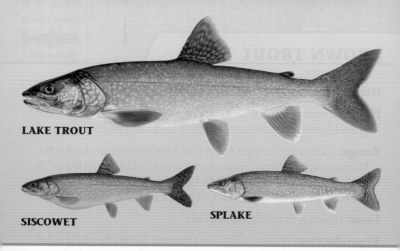

LAKE TROUT

SISCOWET

SPLAKE

Description: dark gray to gray-green on head, back, top fins and tail; white spots on sides and unpaired fins; deeply forked tail; inside of mouth is white

Similar Species: Brook Trout (pg.92), Splake, Siscowet

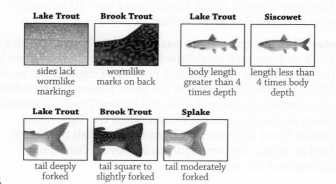

Lake Trout	Brook Trout	Lake Trout	Siscowet
sides lack wormlike markings	wormlike marks on back	body length greater than 4 times depth	length less than 4 times body depth

Lake Trout	Brook Trout	Splake
tail deeply forked	tail square to slightly forked	tail moderately forked

LAKE TROUT

Salvelinus namaycush

Salmonidae

Other Names: togue, mackinaw, great gray trout, laker

Habitat: cold (less than 65 degrees), oxygen-rich waters of deep, clear, infertile lakes

Range: Great Lakes north through Canada, to northeastern U.S., stocked in the Rocky Mountains; deep, cold lakes in the northwest corner of the Lower Peninsula, lakes Superior and Michigan

Food: small fish, insects

Reproduction: females scatter eggs over rocky lake bottoms when fall water temperature falls below 50 degrees

Average Size: 7 to 10 pounds

Records: State—61 pounds, 8 ounces, Lake Superior, 1997; North American—74 pounds, 4 ounces; Great Bear Lake, N.W.T., Canada, 1995

Notes: This native of Michigan can grow very large and is more closely related to char than trout. Lake Trout once supported a large commercial fishery in Lake Michigan, but no longer reproduces naturally in the lake. The population was decimated in the mid-1950s by overfishing and the introduction of the Sea Lamprey. The Lake Michigan lake trout fishery is now maintained by a vigorous stocking program. A high-fat subspecies called the Siscowet (*Salvelinus namaycush siscowet*) or "fat" Lake Trout inhabits the deep waters of Lake Superior and may spend its life in water no warmer than 40 degrees.

Description: blue-green to brown head and back; silver lower sides, often with pink to rose stripe; sides, back, dorsal fins and tail are covered with small black spots

Similar Species: Brown Trout (pg. 94), Brook Trout (pg. 92), Pink Salmon (pg. 104), Chinook Salmon (pg. 100)

Rainbow Trout	**Brown Trout**	**Rainbow Trout**	**Brook Trout**
pinkish stripe on silvery body	sides lack pinkish stripe	lacks wormlike markings	wormlike marks on back

Rainbow Trout	**Pink Salmon**	**Chinook Salmon**
white mouth	dark tongue and jaw tip	black or dark gray mouth

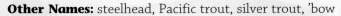

RAINBOW TROUT

Oncorhynchus mykiss

Salmonidae

Other Names: steelhead, Pacific trout, silver trout, 'bow

Habitat: prefers whitewater in cool streams and coastal regions of large lakes, tolerates smaller cool, clear lakes

Range: Pacific Ocean and coastal streams from Mexico to Alaska and northeast Russia, introduced world wide; in Michigan, stocked in many cooler streams and lakes

Food: insects, small crustaceans, and fish

Reproduction: predominantly spring spawners but some strains spawn in fall; females build nest (or redd) in well-aerated gravel in both streams and lakes

Average Size: 20 inches, 3 to 8 pounds

Records: State—26 pounds, 8 ounces, Lake Michigan, 1975; North American—42 pounds, 2 ounces, Bell Island, Alaska, 1970

Notes: The Rainbow Trout was introduced from the Pacific Northwest and is now one of Michigan's most important sport fish. Rainbow Trout are the most adaptable of all the trout and survive well in most cool clear streams and cool lakes where there is not a large sunfish population. Steelhead Trout are rainbows that originally spent some time in the open ocean then interred freshwater streams to spawn. Steelhead stocked in the Great Lakes reside in the lakes, then attempt to spawn in tributary streams.

Description: iridescent green to blue-green back and upper sides, silver below lateral line; small spots on back and tail; inside of mouth is dark; breeding males are olive brown to purple with pronounced kype (hooked snout)

Similar Species: Coho Salmon (pg. 102), Pink Salmon (pg. 104), Rainbow Trout (pg. 98)

Chinook Salmon	Coho Salmon	Pink Salmon
small spots throughout tail	spots only in top half of tail	eye-sized spots throughout tail

Chinook Salmon	Coho Salmon	Rainbow Trout
inside of mouth is dark	inside of mouth is gray	inside of mouth is white

CHINOOK SALMON

Oncorhynchus tshawytscha

Other Names: king, spring salmon, tyee, quinnat, black mouth

Habitat: open ocean and large clear gravel bottomed rivers, open water of lakes Superior and Michigan and associated spawning streams

Range: Pacific Ocean from California to Japan, introduced to the Atlantic coast in Maine; in Michigan found in lakes Superior and Michigan and associated spawning streams

Food: fish (especially smelt and ciscoes), crustaceans

Reproduction: chinooks in the Great Lakes mature in 3 to 5 years; in October and November they migrate up streams to attempt nesting on gravel bars; adults die shortly after

Average Size: 24 to 30 inches, 15 to 20 pounds

Records: State—46 pounds, 1 ounce, Grand River, Kent County, 1978; North American—97 pounds, 4 ounces, Kenai River, Alaska, 1985

Notes: Largest member of the salmon family, chinooks may reach forty pounds in land locked lakes. Prior to the 1960s many unsuccessful attempts were made to introduce Chinook salmon into the Great lakes region. Since 1965, a stable population of hatchery-reared fish have been maintained in lakes Superior and Michigan, creating the most important sport fishery in the state. Michigan chinooks mature in four years and have fall spawning runs.

Description: dark metallic blue to green back; silver sides and belly; small dark spots on back, sides and upper half of tail; inside of mouth is gray; breeding adults gray to green on head with red-maroon on sides, males develop kype (hooked snout)

Similar Species: Chinook Salmon (pg. 100), Pink Salmon (pg. 104), Rainbow Trout (pg. 98)

Coho Salmon	Chinook Salmon	Pink Salmon
spots only in top half of tail	small spots throughout tail	eye-sized spots throughout tail

Coho Salmon	Rainbow Trout
inside of mouth is gray	inside of mouth is white

COHO SALMON
Oncorhynchus kisutch

Other Names: silver salmon, sea trout, blueback

Habitat: open ocean near clear, gravel-bottomed spawning streams, Lake Superior within 10 miles of shore

Range: Pacific Ocean north from California to Japan, Atlantic coast of U.S.; in Michigan, lakes Superior and Michigan and associated tributary spawning streams

Food: smelt, alewives and other fish

Reproduction: spawns in October and November; adults migrate up tributary streams to build nests on gravel bars; parent fish die shortly after spawning

Average Size: 20 inches, 4 to 5 pounds

Records: State—30 pounds, 8 ounces, Platte River, Benzie County, 1976; North American—33 pounds, 4 ounces, Salmon River, New York, 1989

Notes: This Pacific Salmon was first stocked in the Great Lakes by the Michigan DNR in 1965 and has provided the state with a very successful sportfishing industry since the early 1970s. Cohos migrate up streams to spawn in the fall after spending two years in the open lake. The adults die after spawning.

103

Description: steel blue to blue-green back with silver sides; dark spots on back and tail, some as large as the eye; breeding males develop a large hump in front of the dorsal fin and a hooked upper jaw (kype); both sexes are pink during spawn

Similar Species: Chinook Salmon (pg. 100), Coho Salmon (pg. 102), Brown Trout (pg. 94), Rainbow Trout (pg. 98)

Pink Salmon	**Chinook Salmon**	**Coho Salmon**
eye-sized spots throughout tail	small spots throughout tail	spots only in top half of tail

Pink Salmon	**Coho Salmon**	**Brown Trout**	**Rainbow Trout**
dark tongue and jaw tip	inside of mouth is gray	inside of mouth is white	inside of mouth is white

PINK SALMON
Oncorhynchus gorbuscha

Other Names: humpback salmon, humpy, autumn salmon

Habitat: Coastal Pacific Ocean and open water of the Great Lakes, spawns in clear streams

Range: coastal Pacific Ocean from northern California to Alaska, introduced to Great Lakes; rare in Lake Michigan, and thinly distributed in Lake Superior, spawns in a few streams in Michigan's Upper Peninsula

Food: small fish, crustaceans

Reproduction: spawns in fall in tributary streams, usually at two years of age; female builds nest on gravel bar, then covers fertilized eggs; adults die after spawning

Average Size: 17 to 19 inches, 1 to 2 pounds

Records: State—8 pounds, 8 ounces, Carp River, Mackinac County, 1987; North American—12 pounds, 9 ounces, Moose and Kenai Rivers, Alaska, 1974

Notes: This Pacific salmon was unintentionally released into Thunder Bay in 1956 and has since spread throughout the Great Lakes. It spends two to three years in the open lake then moves into streams to spawn and die. Often seen along the lakeshore during the odd-year spawning run, less common in even years. Pink Salmon are not often caught by anglers and are not considered great table fare; the flesh deteriorates rapidly and must be quickly put on ice.

Description: silver with faint pink or purple tinge; dark back; light-colored tail; small mouth; long body but deeper than Rainbow Smelt

Similar Species: Lake Whitefish (pg. 108); Mooneye (pg. 76), Rainbow Smelt (pg. 114)

Cisco	Lake Whitefish	Cisco	Mooneye

| jaws equal length or slight underbite | snout protrudes beyond lower jaw | adipose fin | lacks adipose fin |

Cisco	Rainbow Smelt

| deep body (also inconspicuous teeth) | slim profile (also prominent teeth) |

CISCO

Coregonus artedi

Other Names: shallow water, common or Great Lakes cisco, lake herring, tullibee

Habitat: shoal waters of the Great Lakes and nutrient-poor inland lakes with oxygen-rich depths that remain cool during the summer

Range: northeastern U.S., Great Lakes and Canada; in Michigan, shallow coastal waters of lakes Superior and Michigan, and deep, nutrient-poor inland lakes throughout the state

Food: plankton, small crustaceans, aquatic insects

Reproduction: spawns in November and December when water temperatures reach the lower 30s; eggs are deposited over clean bottoms, usually in 3 to 8 feet of water

Average Size: 10 to 12 inches, 12 ounces

Records: State—5 pounds, 6.4 ounces, Grand Traverse Bay, Grand Traverse County, 1992; North American—7 pounds, 4 ounces, Cedar Lake, Manitoba, 1986

Notes: Ciscoes were once the most productive commercial fish in the Great Lakes. They are still common in Superior but threatened in Lake Michigan. Many "smoked whitefish" sold today are really ciscoes. The inland forms of ciscoes are known as tullibees and vary greatly in size from one lake to another. Ciscoes can be caught through the ice in winter, or by fly-fishermen in the summer.

Description: silver with dark brown to olive back and tail; snout protrudes past lower jaw; mouth is small, with two small flaps between the openings of each nostril

Similar Species: Cisco (pg. 106), Mooneye (pg. 76), Rainbow Smelt (pg. 114)

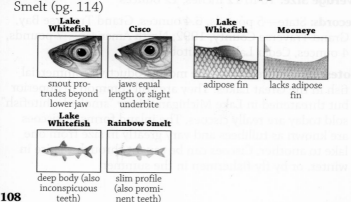

Lake Whitefish	Cisco	Lake Whitefish	Mooneye
snout protrudes beyond lower jaw	jaws equal length or slight underbite	adipose fin	lacks adipose fin

Lake Whitefish	Rainbow Smelt
deep body (also inconspicuous teeth)	slim profile (also prominent teeth)

LAKE WHITEFISH
Coregonus clupeaformis

Other Names: eastern, common or Great Lakes whitefish, gizzard fish, Sault whitefish

Habitat: large, deep, clean inland lakes with cool, oxygen-rich depths during the summer; shallow areas of the Great Lakes

Range: from the Great Lakes north across North America; in Michigan, found mostly in lakes Superior and Michigan, and a few inland lakes in the northeast corner of the state

Food: zooplankton, insects, small fish

Reproduction: spawns on shallow gravel bars in late fall when water temperatures reach the low 30s; occasionally ascends streams to spawn

Average Size: 18 inches, 3 to 5 pounds

Records: State—14 pounds, 4.8 ounces, Lake Superior, 1993; North American—15 pounds, 6 ounces, Clear Lake, Ontario, 1983

Notes: The largest whitefish in North America, the Lake Whitefish was historically the most important food fish in Michigan—first for the Native Americans (the most renowned fishery being at Sault St. Marie), then for early commercial fishermen. The whitefish population was greatly reduced by the 1950s, by debris from the sawmills covering spawning beds, overfishing and the introduction of the Sea Lamprey.

Description: blotchy brown coloration; large mouth; eyes set almost on top of the broad head; large, winglike pectoral fins; lacks scales

Similar Species: Round Goby

Mottled Sculpin	Round Goby
lacks scales	scales on body

MOTTLED SCULPIN

Cottus baridii

Other Names: common sculpin, muddler or gudgeon

Habitat: cool, hard-water streams and clear lakes; favors areas with rocks or vegetation

Range: eastern U.S. through Canada to Hudson Bay and the Rocky Mountains; headwater streams and some lakes in most of Michigan; other types of sculpins are restricted to the northern third of the state, and the Great Lakes

Food: aquatic invertebrates, fish eggs, small fish

Reproduction: spawns in April and May at water temperatures of 63 to 74 degrees; male fans out cavity beneath a rock, ledge or log and attracts females through courtship displays such as head nodding, head shaking and gill cover raising; spawning fish turn upside down and deposit eggs on underside of nest cover; male guards and cleans the nest

Average Size: 4 to 5 inches

Records: none

Notes: Most of the 300 species of sculpins in North America are marine fish. There are a few freshwater species spread across the U.S. and Canada. The Mottled Sculpin is the most common sculpin in Michigan, and is frequently found in trout streams. Sculpins were once thought to prey heavily on trout eggs but several studies have shown this not to be true. The Deepwater Sculpin resides in the deeper portions of the Great Lakes and is an important food source for Lake Trout.

Description: long, thin body; sides bright silver with conspicuous black stripe; upturned mouth; two dorsal fins

Similar Species: Common Shiner (pg. 74), Rainbow Smelt (pg. 114)

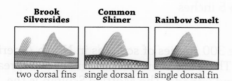

Brook Silversides	Common Shiner	Rainbow Smelt
two dorsal fins	single dorsal fin	single dorsal fin

BROOK SILVERSIDES

Atherinidae

Labidesthes sicculus

Other Names: northern silversides, skipjack, friar

Habitat: surface of clear lakes and large streams

Range: southeastern U.S. to the Great Lakes; common in the clear lakes and larger streams in the southern one-third of Michigan

Food: aquatic and flying insects, spiders

Reproduction: spawns in late spring and early summer; eggs are laid in sticky strings that attach to vegetation; adults die soon after spawning

Average Size: 3 to 4 inches

Records: none

Notes: The Brook Silversides belongs to a large family of fish that is mostly tropical and subtropical, and primarily found in saltwater. It is a flashy fish often seen cruising near the surface in small schools. Its upturned mouth is an adaptation to surface feeding, and it is not uncommon to see a Brook Silversides leap from the water, flying fish style, in pursuit of prey. Because of this tendency to jump, coupled with a lack of hardiness when kept in captivity, it is a poor aquarium fish despite its beauty.

113

Description: large mouth with prominent teeth; jaw extends to rear margin of the eye; dark green back; violet-blue sides and white belly; deeply forked tail; adipose fin

Similar Species: Cisco (pg. 106), Lake Whitefish (pg. 108); Mooneye (pg. 76), Common Shiner (pg. 74), Brook Silversides (pg. 112)

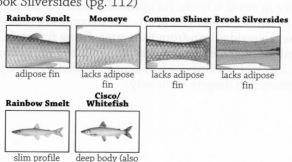

Rainbow Smelt	Mooneye	Common Shiner	Brook Silversides
adipose fin	lacks adipose fin	lacks adipose fin	lacks adipose fin

Rainbow Smelt	Cisco/ Whitefish
slim profile (also prominent teeth)	deep body (also inconspicuous teeth)

RAINBOW SMELT

Osmerus mordax

Other Names: ice or frost fish, lake herring, leefish

Habitat: open oceans and large lakes, tributaries at spawning

Range: Coastal Pacific, Atlantic and Arctic Oceans, land-locked in northeast U.S. and southeast Canada; in Michigan, lakes Superior, Erie, Huron and Michigan, and a few large inland lakes

Food: crustaceans, insect larvae, small fish

Reproduction: spawning takes place in May, at night, in the first mile of tributary streams

Average Size: 8 to 10 inches

Records: none

Notes: Smelt are saltwater fish that enter freshwater to spawn. In 1912 they were successfully introduced into Howe, Crystal and Trout lakes to support the introduced salmon stock. Smelt soon escaped into Lake Michigan and were found in Green Bay in 1924. This small fish was soon making spectacular spawning runs and smelt fishing became a spring ritual. The Great Lakes smelt population crashed in the 1980s and has not fully recovered.

BROOK STICKLEBACK

NINESPINE STICKLEBACK

Description: both Brook and Ninespine Sticklebacks are brown with torpedo-shaped body and very narrow caudal peduncle (area just before the tail); front portion of dorsal fin has short, separated spines; pelvic fins are abdominal and reduced to a single spine; small, sharp teeth

Similar Species: Brook Stickleback, Ninespine Stickleback

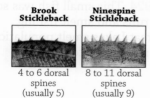

Brook Stickleback	Ninespine Stickleback
4 to 6 dorsal spines (usually 5)	8 to 11 dorsal spines (usually 9)

116

BROOK STICKLEBACK

Gasterosteidae

Culaea inconstans

Other Names: common or many-spined-stickleback, spiny minnow

Habitat: shallows of cool streams and lakes

Range: Kansas through the northern U.S. and Canada; common in cool streams and lakes throughout Michigan

Food: feeds on small aquatic animals, occasionally algae

Reproduction: in water temperatures from 50 to 68 degrees, male builds a golf ball-sized, globular nest of sticks, algae and other plant matter on submerged vegetation; females deposit eggs and depart, often plowing a hole in the side of the nest in the process; the male repairs any damage and viciously guards the eggs until hatching; an ambitious male may build a second, larger nest and transfer the eggs there by mouth

Average Size: 2 to 4 inches

Records: none

Notes: Most members of the stickleback family are marine fish but some are equally at home in fresh- or saltwater. Anglers are is most likely to encounter a Brook Stickleback in the bait pail mixed in with small fatheads or "crappie minnows." Though often discarded in disgust, they do work well as bait. These pugnacious little predators also make fun aquarium fish, and will readily build and defend nests in captivity. Another Stickleback, the Ninespine, is restricted to the Great Lakes.

117

Description: slate gray to brown sides, white belly; bony plates on skin; tail lacks plates and is shark-like, with upper lobe longer than lower; blunt snout with four barbels; spiracles (openings between eye and corner of gill)

Similar Species: Shovelnose Sturgeon

Lake Sturgeon	Shovelnose Sturgeon
spiracle between eye and gill	lacks spiracles

LAKE STURGEON
Acipenser fulvescens

Other Names: rock sturgeon, smoothback

Habitat: quiet waters of large rivers and streams

Range: Hudson Bay, Great Lakes, Mississippi and Missouri drainages southeast to Alabama; in Michigan, lakes Superior, Michigan, Huron and a few large tributary streams

Food: snails, clams, crayfish, aquatic insects

Reproduction: spawns April through June in lake shallows and tributary streams; a single female may produce up to 1 million eggs

Average Size: 20 to 55 inches, 5 to 40 pounds

Records: State—193 pounds, Mullett Lake, Cheboygan County, 1974 (not registered as a North American record); North American—168 pounds, Nattawasaga Lake, Ontario, 1982

Notes: The Lake Sturgeon is the largest fish found in Michigan, and historically reached weights of more than 200 pounds. Michigan's Lake Sturgeons are only found in or near the Great Lakes, not in inland lakes or streams. It is a very primitive fish that has cartilage in place of bones, and bony plates in place of scales. These slow-growing fish don't reproduce until they are twenty years old and may live to be seventy-five or older.

119

Description: slate-green to dark gray back; sides have a blue-bronze sheen; deep-bodied with a sloping back supporting a long dorsal fin; upper lip well below eye

Similar Species: Common Carp (pg. 66)

Black Buffalo

mouth lacks barbels

Common Carp

barbels below mouth

BLACK BUFFALO

Ictiobus niger

Catostomidae

Other Names: buoy tender, current or deep-water buffalo

Habitat: deep, fast water of large streams; deep sloughs, backwaters and impoundments

Range: lower Great Lakes and Mississippi drainages west to South Dakota, south to New Mexico and Louisiana; in Michigan, lakes Michigan, Huron and Erie, and streams in the southern half of the state

Food: aquatic insects, crustaceans, algae

Reproduction: spawning takes place in April and May when fish move up tributaries to lay eggs in flooded sloughs and marshes

Average Size: 10 to 12 pounds

Records: State—32 pounds 3 ounces, Grand River, Ottawa County, 2004; North American—63 pounds, 6 ounces; Mississippi River, Iowa, 1999

Notes: The Bigmouth Buffalo is a southern species that inhabits the deep strong currents of large rivers. They are rare to uncommon in Michigan in what seems to be a population separated from the main Mississippi population. Rarely caught on hook and line, but notable because of their large size. Black Buffalo are one of the largest naturally occurring fish in Michigan.

Description: bright silver, often with yellow tinge; fins clear; deep body with round, blunt head; leading rays of dorsal fin extend into a large, arching "quill"

Similar Species: Common Carp (pg. 66)

Quillback	Common Carp
mouth lacks barbels	barbels below mouth

QUILLBACK

Carpiodes cyprinus

Other Names: silver carp, carpsucker, lake quillback

Habitat: slow-flowing streams and rivers; backwaters and lakes, particularly areas with soft bottoms

Range: south-central Canada through the Great Lakes to the eastern U.S., south through the Mississippi drainage to the Gulf; in Michigan, lakes Michigan, Huron and Erie drainages in the Lower Peninsula

Food: insects, plant matter, decaying material on bottom

Reproduction: ascends tributaries from late spring through early summer; spawns over sand, gravel or mud

Average Size: 14 inches, 1 to 3 pounds

Records: State—8 pounds, Stony Lake, Oceana County, 2000; North American—8 pounds, 13 ounces, Lake Winnebago, Wisconsin, 2003

Notes: There are four species of carpsuckers in North America; the Quillback is the only one that resides in Michigan. Quillbacks are common in many soft-bottom streams and lakes in Michigan, and though reportedly of good flavor are not of much interest to anglers. This pretty, silver fish travels in schools and feeds by filtering through bottom debris.

Description: olive brown to brownish back; sides silver to bronze; white belly; bright red tail; blunt nose; sickle-shaped dorsal fin

Similar Species: Longnose Sucker (pg. 126), White Sucker, (pg. 128)

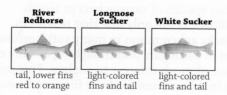

River Redhorse	Longnose Sucker	White Sucker
tail, lower fins red to orange	light-colored fins and tail	light-colored fins and tail

124

RIVER REDHORSE
Moxostoma carinatum

Other Names: redhorse, sucker

Habitat: clean streams and rivers with sand, gravel or rocky bottom; found in a few clear lakes

Range: Great Lake states to New England south to the Gulf; clear, clean streams and a few lakes throughout Michigan

Food: insects, crustaceans, mussels, plant debris

Reproduction: spawns from late May to June in small tributary streams; researchers have observed the male building a 4- to 8-foot-diameter nest on gravel shoal, then courting females by darting back and forth across the nest; a second male may join the display and spawning process

Average Size: 12 to 24 inches, 2 to 10 pounds

Records: State—12 pounds, 14.2 ounces, Muskegon River, Newaygo County, 1991; North American—8 pounds, 11 ounces; Trent River, Ontario, 1997

Notes: There are six species of Redhorse in Michigan, ranging from 2 to 10 pounds. All are "sucker-type fish" rather similar in appearance. They are clean-water fish very susceptible to increased turbidity and pollutants. They are more common in streams but are found in a few lakes. They may all look alike but each is a separate species and occupies its own niche in Michigan waters. Not of sporting importance but the River Redhorse is a fairly common catch for river anglers fishing angleworms on light split shot or slip-sinker rigs on the bottom. Fights well on light tackle.

125

Description: black, brown to dark olive back; slate to pale brown sides fading to white belly; males develop red band during breeding; long snout protruding beyond upper lip

Similar Species: River Redhorse, (pg. 124), White Sucker (pg. 128)

Longnose Sucker	**White Sucker**	**Longnose Sucker**	**River Redhorse**
snout extends well beyond upper lip	snout barely extends past upper lip	fins white to yellowish	fins red to orange

LONGNOSE SUCKER
Catostomus catostomus

Other Names: sturgeon, red or redside sucker

Habitat: primarily shallow waters of large, cold lakes and streams; sometimes found in deeper water

Range: Siberia across Canada through Great Lakes to the eastern U.S.; in Michigan, lakes Superior, Huron, Michigan and their tributaries

Food: small crustaceans, plant material

Reproduction: spawns in April and May, when fish crowd small tributaries

Average Size: 15 to 20 inches, 2 pounds

Records: State—6 pounds, 14 ounces, St. Joseph River, Berrien County, 1986; North American—6 pounds, 14 ounces, St. Joseph River, Michigan, 1986

Notes: This northern, cold-water sucker is the only variety found in both the Old and New World. Thought of as a shallow-water species, it has been netted in depths of up to 600 feet in Lake Superior. Longnose Suckers are rarely taken on hook and line but are netted and speared during the spawning run; they have a fine flavor when smoked.

Description: back is olive, brown or black; sides gray to silver with faint dark patches; white belly; dorsal fin and tail are slate colored; other fins are tinged orange; snout barely extends beyond the upper lip; breeding males develop black and purple bands that can fade within minutes when the fish is handled

Similar Species: Longnose Sucker (pg. 126)

White Sucker	Longnose Sucker
55 to 75 lateral line scales	90 or more scales on lateral line

WHITE SUCKER

Catostomus commersoni

Other Names: common, coarse-scaled or eastern sucker, bay fish, black mullet

Habitat: all permanent waterbodies that can sustain fish

Range: Canada through central and eastern U.S. south to a line from New Mexico to South Carolina; common throughout Michigan in all permanent bodies of water

Food: insects, crustaceans, plant matter

Reproduction: migrates up tributaries in April and May (often until passage is blocked) to spawn in riffles; in large lakes, spawning may occur along shoreline shallows over gravel or coarse sand bottoms

Average Size: 12 to 18 inches, 1 to 3 pounds

Records: State—7 pounds, 3.04 ounces, Au Sable River, Iosco County, 1982; North American—7 pounds, 4 ounces, Big Round Lake, Wisconsin, 1978

Notes: The White Sucker is probably the most common fish in Michigan and the most tolerant of all water conditions. It is commercially harvested for both animal and human consumption, as well as being a mainstay in the bait industry. White Suckers are not the great consumers of trout eggs they were once thought to be, but may compete with trout fry for food when first hatched. However, their tremendous value as a food source for game fish offsets this competition.

Description: dark green back, greenish sides often with dark lateral band; belly white to gray; large, forward-facing mouth; lower jaw extends to rear margin of eye

Similar Species: Smallmouth Bass (pg. 132)

Largemouth Bass	Smallmouth Bass
mouth extends beyond non-red eye	mouth does not extend beyond red eye

SMALLMOUTH BASS

Micropterus dolomieui

Centrarchidae

Other Names: bronzeback, brown or redeye bass, redeye, white or mountain trout

Habitat: clear, swift-flowing streams and rivers; clear lakes with gravel or rocky shorelines

Range: extensively introduced throughout North America; common throughout Michigan, in both the Upper and Lower Peninsula

Food: small fish, crayfish, insects, frogs

Reproduction: in May and June, when water temperature reaches mid- to high 60s, male sweeps out nest in gravel bed, typically in 3 to 10 feet of water; in lakes, nest is often next to a log or boulder—it is below a boulder or other current obstruction in streams; female lays 2,000 to 14,000 eggs; male guards nest and young until fry disperse

Average Size: 12 to 20 inches, 1 to 4 pounds

Records: State—9 pounds, 4 ounces, Long Lake, Cheboygan County, 1906; North American—11 pounds, 15 ounces, Dale Hollow Lake, Tennessee, 1955

Notes: Smallmouth Bass are world-class game fish noted for strong fights and acrobatic jumps. This scrappy fish has been introduced throughout the world as a game fish. It is best known as a fast-water stream fish, but there are good populations in clean lakes, including the shallows of the Great Lakes. The flesh is firm, succulent, and regarded by some anglers as second only to Lake Trout and Whitefish.

Description: black to dark olive back; silver sides with dark green or black blotches; back slightly more arched—and depression above eye less pronounced—than White Crappie

Similar Species: White Crappie (pg. 136)

Black Crappie	White Crappie	Black Crappie	White Crappie
usually 7 to 8 spines in dorsal fin	usually 5 to 6 spines in dorsal fin	dorsal fin length equal to distance from dorsal to eye	dorsal fin shorter than distance from eye to dorsal

BLACK CRAPPIE
Pomoxis nigromaculatus

Other Names: papermouth, speck, speckled perch

Habitat: quiet, clear water of streams and mid-sized lakes; often associated with weedgrowth but may roam deep, open basins and flats, particularly during winter

Range: southern Manitoba through the Atlantic and south-eastern states, introduced in the West; common in all three Michigan drainages

Food: small fish, aquatic insects, zooplankton

Reproduction: spawns in shallow weedbeds from May to June when water temperatures reach the high 50s; male sweeps out circular nest, typically on fine gravel or sand; female may produce more than 180,000 eggs; male guards nest and fry until young crappies are feeding on their own

Average Size: 7 to 12 inches, 10 ounces to 1 pound

Records: State—4 pounds, 2 ounces, Lincoln Lake, Kent County, 1947; North American—6 pounds; Westwego Canal, Louisiana, 1969

Notes: Pursued by Michigan panfish anglers year-round for its sweet-tasting white fillets, it is an aggressive carnivore that will hit everything from waxworms and fatheads to jigging spoons. Not noted as a tremendous fighter, but puts up a good struggle on light tackle. Actively feeds at night. Prefers cleaner water and more vegetation than the White Crappie, and nests in somewhat shallower water.

Description: greenish back; silvery green to white sides with 7 to 9 dark, vertical bars; the only sunfish with six spines in both the dorsal and anal fin

Similar Species: Black Crappie (pg. 134)

White Crappie	Black Crappie	White Crappie	Black Crappie

usually 5 to 6 spines in dorsal fin	usually 7 to 8 spines in dorsal fin	dorsal fin shorter than distance from eye to dorsal	dorsal fin length equal to distance from dorsal to eye

WHITE CRAPPIE

Pomoxis annularis

Other Names: silver, pale or ringed crappie, papermouth

Habitat: slightly silty streams and mid-size lakes; prefers less vegetation than Black Crappie

Range: North Dakota south and east to Gulf and Atlantic, except peninsular Florida; most common in southeastern Michigan; rare to uncommon in the rest of the Lower Peninsula, not found in the U.P.

Food: aquatic insects, small fish, plankton

Reproduction: spawns on firm sand or gravel bottom in May and June when water temperature approaches 60 degrees; male fans out nest, guards eggs and young after spawning

Average Size: 6 to 12 inches, 8 to 16 ounces

Records: State—3 pounds, 6 ounces, Stony Creek Lake, Macomb County, 2000; North American—5 pounds, 3 ounces, Enid Dam, Mississippi, 1957

Notes: White Crappies are the southern cousin to Black Crappies, preferring deeper, less weedy and more turbid (cloudy) water. They have been introduced into a few lakes in the U.P. but are not very successful there. Due to its acceptance of turbid (cloudy) water, there is some indication of a positive relationship between Common Carp and White Crappie. Both Black and White Crappies actively feed during the winter, ensuring that they are the two of the most popular panfish during the ice fishing season.

Description: round, flat body; spines in dorsal and anal fins; small mouth; dark olive to green on back, blending to silver-gray, copper, orange, purple or brown on sides with 5 to 9 dark, vertical bars that may fade with age; yellow underside and copper breast, which intensifies on spawning males; large, dark gill spot; dark spot on rear margin of dorsal fin

Similar Species: Green Sunfish (pg. 140), Pumpkinseed (pg. 146)

Bluegill	Green Sunfish	Bluegill	Pumpkinseed
small mouth	large mouth	dark gill spot	orange crescent

Bluegill	Pumpkinseed
dark spot on dorsal fin	no dark spot

BLUEGILL

Lepomis macrochirus

Centrarchidae

Other Names: 'gill, bull, bream, copperbelly

Habitat: medium to large streams and most lakes with weedy bays or shorelines

Range: southern Canada into Mexico; common throughout Michigan, present but less common in the Upper Peninsula

Food: insects, small fish, leeches, snails, zooplankton, algae

Reproduction: spawns from late May to early August; "parental" male excavates nest in gravel or coarse sand, often in shallow weeds, in colony of up to 50 other nests; often, a smaller "cuckholder" male darts into the nest and fertilizes eggs; parental male guards nest until fry disperse

Average Size: 6 to 9 inches, 5 to 10 ounces

Records: State—2 pounds, 12 ounces, Vaughn Lake, Alcona County, 1983; North American—4 pounds, 12 ounces, Ketona Lake, Alabama, 1950

Notes: Bluegills are the most popular panfish in Michigan and throughout the United States. They have small mouths and feed mostly on insects and small fish. They often feed on the surface and are popular with fly fishermen. Bluegills prefer deep weedbeds at the edge of open water. Many lakes have large populations of hybrid sunfish—crosses between Bluegills and Green, Redear or Pumpkinseed Sunfish.

139

Description: dark green back; dark olive to bluish sides; yellow or whitish belly; scales flecked with yellow, producing a brassy appearance; dark gill spot has a pale margin

Similar Species: Bluegill (pg. 138)

Green Sunfish

large mouth

Bluegill

small mouth

GREEN SUNFISH
Lepomis cyanellus

Other Names: green perch, blue-spotted sunfish, sand bass

Habitat: warm, weedy shallow lakes and the backwaters of slow-moving streams

Range: most of the U.S. into Mexico excluding Florida and the Rocky Mountains; very common in southern Michigan, less so as you move north; rare in the Upper Peninsula

Food: aquatic insects, crustaceans, small fish

Reproduction: beginning in May, male fans out a nest on gravel bottom, often in less than 1 foot of water, near weeds or other cover beneath overhanging limbs; male may grunt to lure female into nest; after spawning, male guards nest and fans eggs; spawns in water temperatures from 60 to 80 degrees and is quite capable of producing two broods per season

Average Size: 5 inches, less than 8 ounces

Records: State—1 pound, 8 ounces, Kirkwood Lake, Oakland County, 1990; North American—2 pounds, 2 ounces, Stockton Lake, Missouri, 1971

Notes: Green Sunfish are often mistaken for Bluegills but prefer shallower weedbeds. They are very common in southern Michigan lakes, though they are completely absent from some water bodies. Green Sunfish stunt easily, filling some lakes with 3-inch-long "potato chips." Green Sunfish hybridize with Bluegills and Pumpkinseeds, producing large, aggressive offspring.

141

Description: small, brightly colored sunfish; sides are flecked with blue or yellow, the belly and chest range from bright orange to pale yellow; gill flap tapers into a long, black finger that is tinged in red

Similar Species: Redear Sunfish (pg. 148)

Northern Longear Sunfish	**Redear Sunfish**	**Northern Longear Sunfish**	**Redear Sunfish**
blue-green bands on side of head	solid green to bronze head	dark spots on dorsal fin	no spots on dorsal fin

NORTHERN LONGEAR SUNFISH

Centrarchidae

Lepomis megalotis

Other Names: Great Lakes longear, blue-and-orange sunfish, red perch

Habitat: clear, moderately weedy, slow-moving shallow streams and clear lakes

Range: central states north to Quebec, then east to the Appalachian Mountains and as far south as the Gulf of Mexico; introduced into some western states; common throughout Michigan's Lower Peninsula

Food: small insects, crustaceans and fish

Reproduction: males build and guard nests on shallow gravel beds when water temperatures reach the mid-70s

Average Size: 3 to 4 inches, 5 ounces

Records: State—no record; North American: 1 pound, 12 ounces, Elephant Butte Lake, New Mexico, 1985

Notes: A colorful but secretive little sunfish, it prefers clear, slow-moving shallow streams—but does inhabit clean lakes. It is a southern species that reaches the limits of its range in the southern Great Lakes region. Longear Sunfish are disappearing from many streams due to increased siltation from agriculture. They feed on the surface more than other sunfish. There is some hybridization between longears and other sunfish.

143

Description: blue-green back fading to orange; about 30 orange or red spots on sides of males, brown spots on females; orange pelvic and anal fins; black gill spot has light margin

Similar Species: Bluegill (pg. 138), Green Sunfish (pg. 140), Redear Sunfish (pg. 148)

Orangespotted Sunfish	Bluegill	Redear Sunfish
light margin on gill spot	gill spot lacks light margin	orange or red crescent on gill

Orangespotted Sunfish	Green Sunfish
hard spines higher than soft rays	hard spines shorter than soft rays

ORANGESPOTTED SUNFISH

Lepomis humilis

Other Names: orangespot, dwarf sunfish, pygmy sunfish

Habitat: open to moderately weedy pools with soft bottoms

Range: southern Great Lakes through Mississippi River basin to Gulf States; in Michigan only found in a few lakes, and tributaries of Lake Erie

Food: insects, crustaceans

Reproduction: male builds and guards nest in shallow water when water temperatures reach mid 60s; colonial nesters

Average Size: 3 to 4 inches, 4 ounces

Records: none

Notes: This brightly colored sunfish is too small to be an important panfish in Michigan. It may be more appropriate as an aquarium fish. However, Orangespotted Sunfish are very abundant in some lakes and are an important forage species for larger game fish. They may also be important for mosquito larvae control in some areas. They survive well in silty water and tolerate slight pollution, making them well suited for small lakes in agricultural areas.

145

Description: back brown to olive; sides speckled with orange, yellow, blue and green spots with 7 to 10 vertical bands; chest and belly yellow or orange; black gill spot has light margin with orange or red crescent

Similar Species: Bluegill (pg. 138), Green Sunfish (pg. 140), Orangespotted Sunfish (pg. 144)

Pumpkinseed	Bluegill	Orangespotted Sunfish
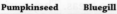		
orange or red crescent on gill flap	gill spot lacks light margin	light margin on gill spot

Pumpkinseed	Green Sunfish
long, pointed pectoral fin	rounded pectoral fin

PUMPKINSEED

Lepomis gibbosus

Other Names: 'seed, punky, yellow or round sunfish, bream

Habitat: weedy ponds, clear lakes, reservoirs and slow-moving streams; prefers slightly cooler water than Bluegill

Range: native to eastern and central North America, widely introduced elsewhere; in Michigan, widely distributed in both the Upper and Lower peninsulas and in all four Great Lakes

Food: insects, snails, fish, leeches, small amounts of vegetation

Reproduction: from late May to August starting when water temperatures reach 55 to 63 degrees, male builds nest on gravel bottom among weeds in less than 2 feet of water; nests are located in colonies, often with other sunfish species; female leaves after spawning; male aggressively guards the nest; multiple broods per year common

Average Size: 6 to 8 inches, 6 to 10 ounces

Records: State—1 pound, 5.44 ounces, Baw Beese Lake, Hillsdale County, 2004; North American—2 pounds, 4 ounces, North Saluda River, South Carolina, 1997

Notes: This small, brightly colored sunfish is one of the most common and beautiful panfish caught in Michigan. Pumpkinseeds often gather in small schools around docks and submerged deadfalls. They prefer slightly cooler water than Bluegills and are infrequently found in open water. They readily hybridize with other sunfish and the hybrids may totally colonize some lakes.

147

Description: back and sides are bronze to dark green, fading to a lighter green, with faint vertical bars; the gill flap is short with a dark spot tinged in red on males; bluish stripes on the side of the head

Similar Species: Longear Sunfish, Redear Sunfish

Redear Sunfish	Northern Longear Sunfish	Redear Sunfish	Northern Longear Sunfish
solid green to bronze head	blue-green bands on side of head	no spots on dorsal fin	dark spots on dorsal fin

REDEAR SUNFISH

Lopomis microlophus

Other Names: shellcracker, stumpknocker, yellow bream

Habitat: congregates around stumps and logs in low to moderate vegetation; redears prefer large, quiet lakes but are often introduced into farm ponds

Range: northern Midwest through southern U.S.; introduced into some northern and western states such as Michigan and New Mexico; introduced in the southern third of Michigan's Lower Peninsula

Food: mainly mollusks

Reproduction: males build and guard nests in shallow water in May and June, but may reproduce well into the summer

Average size: 8 to 10 inches, 1 pound

Records: State—1 pound, 15.5 ounces, Thompson Lake, Saint Joseph County, 2002; North American: 5 pounds, 7.5 ounces, Diversion Canal, South Carolina, 1998

Notes: The Redear Sunfish is a large, highly regarded panfish of the South that has been introduced into some northern and western states. The first introduction in Michigan was in the 1950s. More introductions took place in the '80s and a management plan was established in 1991. The introductions have been very successful, with Redears becoming the dominant panfish and a popular panfish in some lakes in the southern part of state. During the winter, anglers target them by dropping small jigs down weed stalks, upon which the Redears hunt for tiny food items.

149

Description: brown to olive green back and sides with dark spots and overall bronze appearance; red eye; thicker, heavier body than other sunfish; large mouth

Similar Species: Bluegill (pg. 138), Green Sunfish (pg. 140), Pumpkinseed (pg. 146), Warmouth (pg. 152)

Rock Bass	Green Sunfish	Pumpkinseed	Warmouth
solid dark gill spot	light margin on gill spot	orange or red crescent on gill flap	dark gill spot with light margin

Rock Bass	Bluegill
large mouth extends to eye	small mouth does not extend to eye

ROCK BASS

Ambloplites rupestris

Other Names: redeye, goggle eye, rock sunfish

Habitat: vegetation on firm to rocky bottom in clear-water lakes and medium-size streams

Range: southern Canada through central and eastern U.S. to northern edge of Gulf states; common throughout Michigan

Food: prefers crayfish, but eats aquatic insects and small fish

Reproduction: spawns in spring at water temperatures from high 60s to 70s; male fans out nest on coarse gravel bottom in weeds less than 3 feet deep; male guards eggs and fry

Average Size: 8 to 10 inches, 8 ounces to 1 pound

Records: State—3 pounds, 10 ounces, Holloway Reservoir, Gennesee County, 1965; North American—3 pounds, York River, Ontario, 1974

Notes: A common sunfish in clear lakes and streams. It is plentiful and a good fighter often caught but not often sought by fishermen. Its flesh is somewhat stronger flavored than that of Bluegills. Rock Bass prefer vegetation that is associated with rocky or gravel substrate, and are frequently found in schools that stay put, not moving from their home territories. Once these schools are located, Rock Bass are easy to catch.

Description: back and sides greenish gray to brown; lightly mottled with faint vertical bands; stout body; large mouth; red eye; 3 to 5 reddish-brown streaks radiate from eye

Similar Species: Bluegill (pg. 138), Green Sunfish (pg. 140), Pumpkinseed (pg. 146), Rock Bass (pg. 150)

Warmouth	Bluegill	Green Sunfish
jaw extends at least to middle of eye	small mouth does not extend to eye	jaw does not extend to middle of eye

Warmouth	Pumpkinseed	Rock Bass
light margin on gill spot	prominent orange or red crescent on gill spot	dark gill spot lacks light margin

WARMOUTH

Lepomis gulosus

Other Names: goggle-eye, wide-mouth sunfish, stumpknocker, weed bass

Habitat: heavy weeds in turbid (cloudy) lakes, reservoirs and slow-moving streams

Range: southern U.S. from Texas to Florida north to the southern Great Lakes region; found in all three Great Lake drainages in the southern half of Michigan

Food: small fish, insects, snails, crustaceans

Reproduction: not a colonial nester like other sunfish; male fans out solitary bed in dense, shallow weeds when water temperatures reach the low 70s; nest is located by a rock, stump or weed clump; male guards eggs after spawning

Average Size: 11 inches, 8 to 12 ounces

Records: State—1 pound, 6 ounces, Great Bear Lake, Van Buren County, 2001; North American—2 pounds, 7 ounces, Yellow River, Florida, 1985

Notes: The Warmouth is a southern panfish that reaches its northern limit in mid-Michigan. More tolerant of turbid (cloudy) water than other Michigan sunfish, Warmouths inhabit warm, shallow lakes and slow-moving streams. They are solitary fish that prefer dense weedbeds to open water. It is a strong, aggressive fish that primarily eats small fish. In lakes lacking dense vegetation, Warmouths may be found clustered near submerged stumps and logs.

153

Description: bright silver; 6 to 8 distinct, uninterrupted black stripes on each side; front hard-spined portion of dorsal fin separated from soft-rayed rear section; lower jaw protrudes beyond snout

Similar Species: Yellow Bass

White Bass	Yellow Bass	White Bass	Yellow Bass

lower jaw protrudes beyond snout	lower jaw even with snout	stripes continuous	stripes broken above anal fin

WHITE BASS

Morone chrysops

Moronidae

Other Names: silver bass, streaker, lake bass, sand bass

Habitat: large lakes, rivers and impoundments with relatively clear water

Range: Great Lakes region to the eastern seaboard, through the southeast to the Gulf, west to Texas; in Michigan, common in Lake Erie, St Clair and Huron particularly Saginaw Bay, less common in the Lake Michigan drainage

Food: small fish

Reproduction: spawns in late spring to early summer at water temperatures of 55 to 79 degrees, in open water over gravel beds or rubble 6 to 10 feet deep; a single female may produce more than 500,000 eggs

Average Size: 18 inches, 8 ounces to 2 pounds

Records: State—6 pounds, 7.04 ounces, Saginaw Bay, Arenac County, 1989; North American—6 pounds, 7 ounces; Saginaw Bay, Michigan, 1989

Notes: The White Bass is a big-lake and river fish and is not found inland in Michigan. It is considered a panfish and highly regarded by anglers. White Bass travel in large "packs" near the surface and can often be spotted by watching for seagulls feeding over the schools. Often anglers gather in large numbers along streams during the White Bass spawning run. It has a good flavor that can be improved if the fish is put on ice and chilled as soon as it is caught.

Description: olive to blackish green back, fading to silver-green on the sides; no black stripes on the sides of adult fish; two dorsal fins touch but are separated

Similar Species: White Bass (pg. 154), Yellow Bass

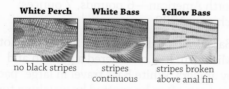

White Perch — no black stripes

White Bass — stripes continuous

Yellow Bass — stripes broken above anal fin

WHITE PERCH
Morone americana

Percichthyidae

Other Names: narrow-mouth bass, silver or sea perch

Habitat: brackish water in coastal areas, coastal areas of the Great Lakes

Range: invading the Mississippi River drainage south to the Gulf of Mexico; in Michigan, lakes Michigan, Huron, Erie and St. Clair

Food: fish eggs in spring and early summer; minnows, insects and crustaceans

Reproduction: spawning takes place late spring over gravel bars of tributary streams

Average Size: 6 to 8 inches, 1 pound or less

Records: State—1 pound, 11 ounces, Lake Huron, Tuscola County, 2002; North American—4 pounds, 12 ounces, Messalonskee Lake, Maine, 1949

Notes: The White Perch is a coastal Atlantic species that entered the Great Lakes in the 1950s and by the mid-'80s reached the Michigan waters of the Great Lakes. In 1988 it was found in the Chicago area and from there has moved into the Upper Mississippi River system. Fish eggs comprise 100 percent the White Perch's diet in the spring and the species has been linked to Walleye declines in some Canadian waters. White Perch are a popular panfish in some parts of the Great Lakes and are commercially harvested in Lake Erie.

157

Description: overall silvery, almost transparent appearance; mottled brown, tan or greenish with dark spots on sides; adipose fin; single dorsal fin with two spines and 10 to 11 rays

Similar Species: Yellow Perch (pg. 84); Walleye (pg. 82)

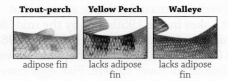

Trout-perch	Yellow Perch	Walleye
adipose fin	lacks adipose fin	lacks adipose fin

TROUT-PERCH

Percopsis omiscomaycus

Other Names: grounder, sand minnow

Habitat: prefers clear to slightly turbid (cloudy) water over sand or gravel; avoids soft-bottomed shallows

Range: east-central U.S. through Canada to Alaska; in Michigan, Trout-perch are found in the Great Lakes and their direct tributaries, not inland

Food: insects, copepods, small fish

Reproduction: spawns from May to August over sand bars and rocks in lakes, or in tributary streams on gravel or sand; two or three males cluster around female, which releases 200 to 700 eggs; fertilized eggs sink to bottom and receive no parental care

Average Size: 3 to 5 inches

Records: none

Notes: There are only two species of Trout-perch and they are restricted to the freshwater of North America. Michigan's lone Trout-perch is a deep-water fish that is seldom seen unless it washes up on a beach (when it is sometimes confused with small walleyes). They do have a nocturnal migration and on some nights large numbers move into the shallows to feed. Trout-perch are an important forage species for game fish and would be a good baitfish. However, seining is only productive in shallow water at night.

GLOSSARY

adipose fin a small, fleshy fin without rays, located on the midline of the fish's back between the dorsal fin and the tail

air bladder a balloon-like organ located in the gut area of a fish, used to control buoyancy—and in the respiration of some species such as gar; also called "swim bladder" or "gas bladder"

alevin a newly hatched fish that still has its yolk sac

anadromous a fish that hatches in freshwater, migrates to the ocean, then re-enters streams or rivers from the sea (or large inland body of water) to spawn

anal fin a single fin located on the bottom of the fish near the tail

annulus marks or rings on the scales, spine, vertebrae or otoliths that scientists use to determine a fish's age

anterior toward the front of a fish, opposite of posterior

bands horizontal marks running lengthwise along the side of a fish

barbel thread-like sensory structures on a fish's head often near the mouth, commonly called "whiskers;" used for taste or smell

bars vertical markings on the side of a fish

benthic organisms living in or on the bottom

brood swarm large group of young fish such as bullheads

cardiform teeth small teeth on the lips of a catfish

carnivore a fish that feeds on other fish or animals

catadromous a fish that lives in freshwater and migrates into salt-water to spawn, such as the American Eel

caudal fin tail fin

160

caudal peduncle the portion of the fish's body located between the anal fin and the beginning of the tail

coldwater referring to a species or environment; in fish, often a species of trout or salmon found in water that rarely exceeds 70 degrees; also used to describe a lake or river according to average summer temperature

copepod a small (less than 2 mm) crustacean that is part of the zooplankton community

crustacean a crayfish, water flea, crab or other animal belonging to group of mostly aquatic species that have paired antennae, jointed legs and an exterior skeleton (exoskeleton); common food for many fish

dorsal relating to the top of the fish, on or near the back; opposite of the ventral, or lower, part of the fish

dorsal fin the fin or fins located along the top of a fish's back

eddy a circular water current, often created by an obstruction

epilimnion the warm, oxygen-rich upper layer of water in a thermally stratified lake

exotic a foreign species, not native to a watershed

fingerling a juvenile fish, generally 1 to 10 inches in length, in its first year of life

fork length the overall length of a fish from the mouth to the deepest part of the tail notch

fry recently hatched young fish that have absorbed their yolk sacs

game fish a species regulated by laws for recreational fishing

gills organs used in aquatic respiration

gill cover large bone covering the gills, also called opercle or operculum

gill raker a comblike projection from the gill arch

harvest fish that are caught and kept by sport or commercial anglers

hypolimnion bottom layer of water in a thermally stratified lake (common in summer), usually depleted of oxygen by decaying matter

ichthyologist a scientist who studies fish

invertebrates animals without backbones, such as insects, crayfish, leeches and earthworms

lateral line a series of pored scales along the side of a fish that contain organs used to detect vibrations

littoral zone the part of a lake that is less than 15 feet in depth; this important and often vulnerable area holds the majority of aquatic plants, is a primary area used by young fish, and offers essential spawning habitat for most warmwater fishes such as Walleye and Largemouth Bass

mandible lower jaw

maxillary upper jaw

milt semen of a male fish that fertilizes the female's eggs during spawning

mollusk an invertebrate with a smooth, soft body such as a clam and snail

native an indigenous or naturally occurring species

omnivore a fish or animal that eats plants and animal matter

otolith an L-shaped bone found in the inner ear of fish

opercle bone covering the gills, also called gill cover or operculum

panfish small freshwater game fish that can be fried whole in a pan, such as crappies, perch and sunfish

pectoral fins paired fins on the side of the fish just behind the gills

pelagic fish species that live in open water, in the food-rich upper layer of water; not associated with the bottom

pelvic fins paired fins below or behind the pectoral fins on the bottom (ventral portion) of the fish

pharyngeal teeth tooth-like structures in the throat on the margins of the gill bars

pheremone a chemical scent secreted as a means of communication between members of the same species

piscivore a predatory fish that mainly eats other fish

planktivore a fish that feeds on plankton

plankton floating or weakly swimming aquatic plants and animals, including larval fish, that drift with the current; often eaten by fish; individual organisms are called plankters

plankton bloom a marked increase in the amount of plankton due to favorable conditions such as nutrients and light

range the geographic region in which a species is found

ray hard supporting part of the fin; resembles a spine but is jointed (can be raised and lowered) and is barbed; found in catfish, carp and goldfish

ray soft flexible structures supporting the fin membrane, sometimes branched

redd a nest-like depression made by a male or female fish during the spawn, often refers to nest of trout and salmon species

riparian area land adjacent to streams, rivers, lakes and other wetlands where the vegetation is influenced by the great availability of water

riprap rock or concrete used to protect a lake shore or river bank from erosion

roe fish eggs

scales small, flat plates covering the outer skin of many fish

Secchi disk a black-and-white circular disk used to measure water clarity; scientists record the average depth at which the disk disappears from sight when lowered into the water

silt small, easily disturbed bottom particles smaller than sand but larger than clay

siltation the accumulation of soil particles

spawning the process of fish reproduction; involves females laying eggs and males fertilizing them to produce young fish

spine stiff, pointed structures found along with soft rays in some fins; unlike hard rays they are not jointed

spiracle an opening on the posterior portion of the head above and behind the eye

standard length length of the fish from the mouth to the end of the vertebral column

stocking the purposeful, artificial introduction of a fish species into an area

substrate bottom composition of a lake, stream or river

subterminal mouth below the snout of the fish

swim bladder see air bladder

tailrace area immediately downstream of a dam or power plant

tapetum lucidum reflective pigment in a Walleye's eye

thermocline middle layer of water in a stratified lake, typically oxygen rich, characterized by a sharp drop in water temperature; often the lowest depth at which fish can be routinely found

terminal mouth forward facing

total length the length of the fish from the mouth to the tail compressed to its fullest length

tributary a stream that feeds into another stream, river or lake

turbid cloudy; water clouded by suspended sediments or plant matter that limits visibility and the passage of light

velocity the speed of water flowing in a stream or river

vent the opening at the end of the digestive tract

ventral the underside of the fish

vertebrate an animal with a backbone

vomerine teeth teeth on the roof of the mouth

warmwater a non-salmonid species of fish that lives in water that routinely exceeds 70 degrees; also used to describe a lake or river according to average summer temperature

yolk the part of an egg containing food for the developing fish

zooplankton the animal component of plankton; tiny animals that float or swim weakly; common food of fry and small fish

PRIMARY REFERENCES

Bailey, R. M. and W. C. Latta, G. R. Smith. 2004
An Atlas of Michigan Fishes
University of Michigan Press

Becker, G. C. 1983
Fishes of Wisconsin
University of Wisconsin Press

Eddy, S. and J. C. Underhill. 1974
Northern Fishes
University of Minnesota Press

Hubbs, C. L. and K. F. Lagler. 1958
Fishes of the Great Lakes Region
University of Michigan Press

McClane, A. J. 1978
Freshwater Fishes of North America
Henry Holt and Company

Phillips, Gary L. and W. D. Schmidt, J. C. Underhill. 1982
Fishes of the Minnesota Region
University of Minnesota Press

INDEX

167

169

R

Rainbow Smelt, 114

Rainbow Trout, 98

Razorback, see: Smallmouth Buffalo

Red, or Redside Sucker, see: Longnose Sucker

Red Cat, see: Brown Bullhead

Redbelly, see: Northern Redbelly Dace

Redeye, see: Rock, Smallmouth Bass

Redeye Bass, see: Smallmouth Bass

Redhorse, see: River Redhorse

Redhorse, River, 124

Redtail, see: Hornyhead Chub

Ringed Crappie, see: White Crappie

Ringed Perch, see: Yellow Perch

River Chub, see: Hornyhead Chub

River Herring, see: Alewife

River Pike, see: Sauger

River Redhorse, 124

River Whitefish, see: Mooneye

Rock Bass, 150

Rock Sturgeon, see: Lake Sturgeon

Rock Sunfish, see: Rock Bass

Round Buffalo, see: Bigmouth Buffalo

Round Sunfish, see: Pumpkinseed

S

Salmon, Chinook, 100

Salmon, Coho, 102

Salmon, Pink, 104

Sand Bass, see: Green Sunfish; White Bass

Sand Pike, see: Sauger

Sand Sturgeon, see: Shovelnose Sturgeon

Sauger, 80

Sault Whitefish, see: Lake Whitefish

Sculpin, Mottled, 110

Sea Lamprey, 62

Sea Perch, see: White Perch

Sea Trout, see: Coho Salmon

'Seed, see: Pumpkinseed

Shad, Gizzard, 58

Shallow Water Cisco, see: Cisco

Sheepshead, see: Freshwater Drum

Shiner, Common, 74

Shiner, Golden, 74

Shortbilled Gar, see: Shortnose Gar

Shovelhead, see: Flathead Catfish

Silver Bass, see: White Bass

Silver Carp; also see: Quillback

ABOUT THE AUTHOR

Dave Bosanko was born in Kansas and studied engineering before following his love of nature to degrees in biology and chemistry from Emporia State University. He spent thirty years as staff biologist at two of the University of Minnesota's field stations. Though his training was in mammal physiology, Dave worked on a wide range of research projects ranging from fish, bird and mammal population studies to experiments with biodiversity and prairie restoration. An avid fisherman and naturalist, he has long enjoyed applying the fruits of his extensive field research to patterning fish location and behavior, and observing how these fascinating species interact with one another in the underwater web of life.